Ultimate
First
Encyclopedia

KINGFISHER
Kingfisher Publications Plc
New Penderal House
283-288 High Holborn
London WC1V 7HZ

First published by Kingfisher Publications Plc 1998

This edition produced for
The Book People Ltd,
Hall Wood Avenue,
Haydock,
St Helens
WA11 9UL

10 9 8 7 6 5 4 3 2 1

Copyright © Kingfisher Publications Plc 1998

A CIP catalogue record for this book is available
from the British Library.

ISBN 0 7534 0302 1

Printed in Singapore

Material previously published in the *First
Encyclopedia*, the *First Science Encylopedia* and
the *First Animal Encyclopedia*.

Material from *First Animal Encyclopedia*
produced for Kingfisher by Warrender
Grant Publications Ltd

Editors: Samantha Armstrong, Sue Barraclough,
Tara Benson, Charlotte Evans, Debbie Fox,
Jenny Vaughn

Designers: Ana Baillarguet, Kelly Flynn, Steven
Laurie, Siân Williams

Art editors: Sue Aldworth, David Noon,
Val Wright

US editor: Aimee Johnson

Proofreaders: Jane Birch, Jill Somerscales,
Nikky Twyman

Photography: Nick Goodall, Lyndon Parker,
Tim Ridley, Andy Teare
Prop organizers: Michelle Callan, Sarah Wilson

DTP operators: Primrose Burton, Tracey
McNerney

Picture research: Veneta Bullen, Nic Dean,
Image Select

Artwork archivist: Wendy Allison
Assistant artwork archivist: Steve Robinson

Production Manager: Sue Wilmot
Production controllers: Richard Waterhouse,
Caroline Jackson
US production manager: Oonagh Phelan

Writers: Anne Civardi, John Farndon,
Anita Ganeri, Jon Kirkwood, Chris Oxlade,
Ruth Thomson

Consultants: John and Sue Becklake, Michael
Chinery, Andrew Kemp, Keith Lye, Peter Mellett,
James Muirden, Dr Elizabeth McCall Smith, Tom
Schiele, Julia Stanton, Toby Stark, Philip Steele,
Dr David Unwin

Ultimate First Encyclopedia:
Cover design: Mike Buckley
Editor: Julie Ferris
Index: Sylvia Potter

Ultimate

First
Encyclopedia

TED SMART

Contents

Your book

Your *Ultimate First Encyclopedia* is packed with exciting information, amazing facts and colourful pictures. All your favourite topics appear in alphabetical order. This page will show you how to use your book.

◁ Information is written above, below or next to each picture. Use the arrows to find out which picture to look at.

▷ Look out for the numbered pictures. The numbers will help you to look at the pictures in the right order.

 1　2  3

**viewfinder
(you look through this)**

shutter release button

◁ Some pictures show things that have many different parts, such as this camera. Labels show you what each part is called.

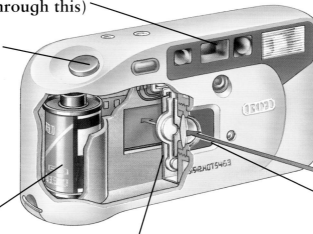

Fact box
• These boxes contain extra information, facts and figures.

film

shutter

lens

**This Sign means
DANGER!
TAKE CARE!**

Find out more
If you want to find out more about each topic, look at this box. It will tell you which pages to look at.

◁ This little person is telling you to move on to the next page.

Acid

Acids are chemicals. Many fruits contain acids. Vinegar and lemon juice are acids, too. These are weak acids. They make things taste sour.

Some acids are strong and can eat away at things. They are dangerous because they burn. But they can be useful. For example, some strong acids are used in making plastics. You have strong acids in your stomach to help you digest your food.

△ **1** You can find out if a substance is an acid. Ask an adult to chop some red cabbage and put it into hot water. Let it cool, then pour the liquid into clean glasses.

△ **2** To test a substance, mix it with some of the cabbage water. Acids turn the cabbage water red. What happens when you test lemon juice? Now try baking soda. This is an alkali, which means it is the opposite of an acid. Alkalis turn the cabbage water green.

▷ Lemons contain an acid called citric acid. This gives the lemon its sharp taste.

Strong acids are dangerous. They can burn.

◁ These trees have been killed by acid rain. Acid rain forms when gases made by burning fuels, such as coal, mix with drops of water in the air. This makes a weak acid, which harms plants and eats away at rocks and buildings.

Find out more
Air and Atmosphere
Chemistry and Chemicals
Fuels

Africa

Africa is the second largest and the warmest continent in the world. It has hot deserts, thick rainforests and flat grasslands where many animals live. Many different peoples live in Africa. Most Africans live in the countryside and are farmers, but more and more are moving to the cities to find work.

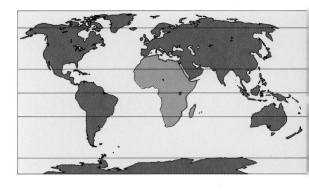

△ On this map, Africa is shown in red. Africa is joined to Asia and a thin sea separates it from Europe.

▽ This man sells water to thirsty people who pass by. Water is very valuable in the desert.

◁ The Sahara is the world's biggest desert. It covers nearly one third of Africa. It also has the highest sand dunes in the world.

△ Cairo is the capital city of Egypt. It is also the largest city in Africa. It is a dusty and crowded city with lots of traffic.

▷ In many villages, women share the work of preparing meals together. Here they are pounding maize into flour to make pancakes.

▷ Many of the world's finest diamonds come from South Africa. They are found buried deep inside rocks.

▷ This beautiful bottle is made out of a gourd, a plant like a pumpkin. It was made in Kenya and has a stopper shaped like a head.

▷ Africa's large grasslands are home to many animals, like these elephants. People also graze cattle on the grassland.

△ Maputo is the capital city of Mozambique in south-east Africa. It has many high-rise buildings and a busy port.

Find out more
Art
Grasslands
History
Water
World

Air and Atmosphere

You cannot see air, but you can feel it when the wind blows. Air is a mixture of different gases. The main ones are nitrogen and oxygen. There is a blanket of air all around the Earth, called the atmosphere.

thermosphere

mesosphere

stratosphere

troposphere

meteor shower

△ The air in the atmosphere gets thinner the farther it gets from the Earth's surface. Each layer has a name.

▽ When we breathe, we take in air. Our bodies need the oxygen in the air to stay alive. We breathe out carbon dioxide as waste. Plants take in carbon dioxide, which they need to make food. They give out oxygen as waste.

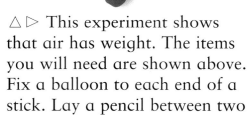

△▷ This experiment shows that air has weight. The items you will need are shown above. Fix a balloon to each end of a stick. Lay a pencil between two cans and balance the stick across it. Mark the stick where it crosses the pencil. Now blow up one of the balloons. Fix it back in place, making sure that the mark on the stick is still over the pencil. Do you know why the stick doesn't balance?

Fact box

• A layer of ozone gas in the atmosphere protects living things from the Sun's harmful rays.

• The air in a bedroom weighs about the same as you do.

Find out more

Earth
Gases
Living things
Weather

12

Albatross

Albatrosses are the biggest of all sea birds. They live in the cold Southern Hemisphere, where they survive on fish and seawater. Albatrosses can glide for great distances on their huge wings, and are able to fly 15,000 kilometres in a single trip over the ocean.

△ The albatross has the longest wings of any bird – nearly four metres from tip to tip. It often flies without flapping its wings at all. Instead, it skims close to the waves and uses the wind to help it along.

▽ Albatrosses only return to land to raise their young. When the young birds are ten months old, they leave the island where they were born and will stay at sea for several years.

Fact box
• Albatross eggs take 80 days to hatch – longer than any other species of bird.
• To feed, albatrosses settle on the sea and catch squid.
• The albatrosses can travel as far as 800km in just 12 hours.

Find out more
Bird
Gull
Penguin
Sea bird

Alligator and Crocodile

Alligators and crocodiles are large reptiles that live in rivers and swamps in tropical areas. They float beneath the surface of the water, with only their eyes and nostrils showing, ready to snap up fish, turtles, and even big mammals in their huge jaws.

△ Crocodiles are cold-blooded creatures that spend much of their lives in the water, keeping cool and hunting. The rest of their time is spent on the riverbank, soaking up the sun's rays. This helps to give them energy.

◁▽ The American alligator (left) has a broader and shorter jaw than the crocodile (below). Both alligators and crocodiles have between 60 and 80 teeth in their powerful jaws. They use the teeth to rip their prey to pieces.

Fact box

• Crocodiles have existed for over 200 million years.
• Alligators can grow up to six metres long.
• The largest, the saltwater crocodile, grows to almost eight metres.

▽ Alligators and crocodiles lay up to 90 eggs in a nest on the riverbank made from mud and leaves. When the young hatch, they call to their mother. She digs them out, picks them up gently in her mouth, and carries them down to the water.

Find out more

Lizard

Amphibian

Amphibians are animals that live both in the water and on the land. Frogs, toads, newts and caecilians are all amphibians. They are found everywhere except Antarctica, particularly in warm places.

△ Newts have long tails and four short legs, and they look like lizards. However, they do not have scales and their skin is moist.

△ Adult frogs and toads have four legs and no tail. Some frogs inflate their throats to make a loud croak. This helps them to attract a mate.

▷ Caecilians have no legs and resemble worms. They live underground in tropical places. Unlike most amphibians, the female caecilian guards her eggs.

◁ **1** A home-made mini-pond is a great way of attracting frogs and newts to your garden. You will need a washing-up bowl, some sand, pondweed, and a few stones and rocks.

◁ **2** Dig a hole in a corner of your garden and drop the bowl into it. Cover the bottom with the sand and stones, making sure that some of the rocks rise above the surface of the water. Add the pondweed, then fill the bowl with water. Over the next few weeks, watch to see if your pond has any visitors.

Find out more
Fish
Frog and Toad
Lizard
Reproduction

Animals

Animals are living things that get their energy to move and grow from eating food. They are all shapes and sizes – from enormous whales to animals so tiny that thousands would fit on to a teaspoon. Some animals even live inside other animals and plants. Animals can be found all over the world – in hot, dry deserts, in icy oceans and on freezing cold mountaintops.

△ This animal is so small that it can be seen only through a microscope.

▽ Blue whales are the biggest animals that ever lived on Earth. Adult blue whales are larger than any of the dinosaurs ever were.

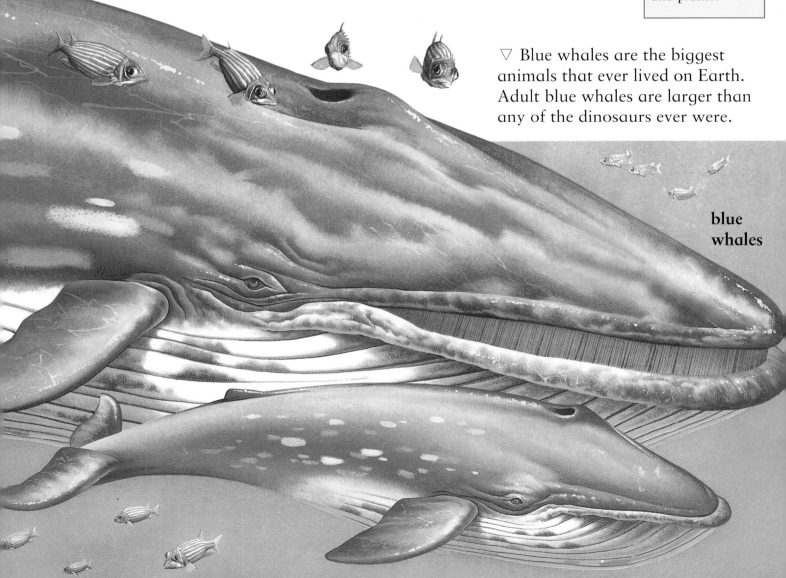

blue whales

Animals in the air
Most animals that have wings can fly. Moths and bats usually fly around at night. Falcons and most other birds fly in the daytime to find food. Falcons swoop down to catch prey.

moth

falcon

long-eared bat

Animals on land
Stocky wombats shuffle slowly. They go into underground burrows if they are scared. Zebras are able to gallop away from danger. Snakes can slither quickly across the ground.

coral snake

wombats

zebra

Animals in water
Jellyfish pump water through their bodies to push themselves along. Crabs scuttle sideways across the sea bed. Fish swim along by moving their tails from side to side.

jellyfish

angel fish

crab

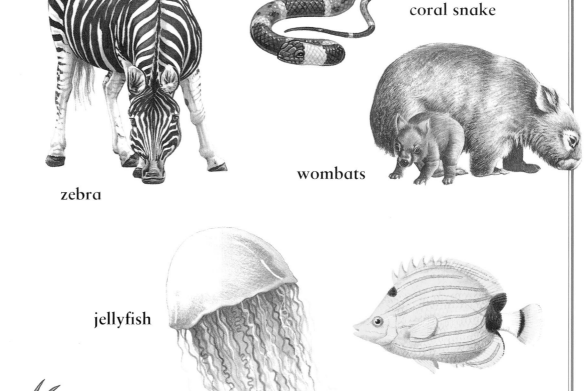

Vertebrates
Animals that have a backbone
are called vertebrates.

gila
monster

△ **Reptiles** are
cold-blooded. They
need heat from the Sun
to keep warm.

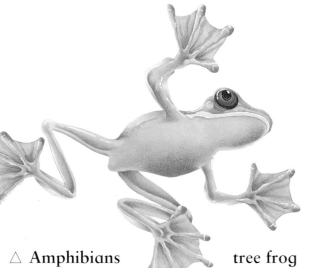

△ **Amphibians**
can live in the
water and on land.
They usually lay their eggs in
water, but spend most of their
time on land.

tree frog

monkey

stickleback

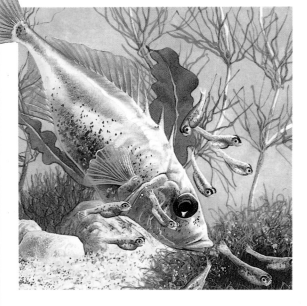

△ **Mammals** usually
have hair or fur to keep
them warm. Babies are cared
for by their mothers and feed
on their mothers' milk.

△ **Fish** live in water. They breathe
with gills, which are slits just
behind their heads. Their bodies
are covered in tiny scales.

hummingbird

◁ **Birds** are
covered with
feathers and
have wings. Most
birds can fly. All
birds have beaks,
or bills, instead
of teeth.

Invertebrates

Animals without backbones are called invertebrates.

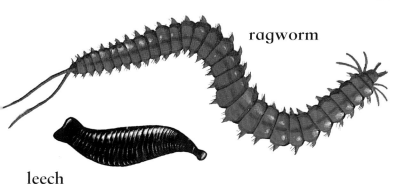

ragworm

leech

lobster

ladybird

△ **Worms** have long, thin, soft bodies with no legs. Their bodies are made up of segments.

△ These **jointed-legged animals** have tough outer skins to protect their soft bodies. Their legs are jointed, like a suit of armour, so that they can move.

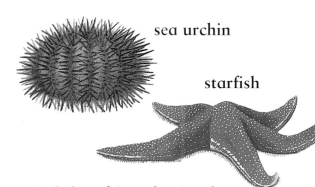

sea urchin

starfish

▷ These **jelly-like animals** live in the sea. They have stinging tentacles for catching food and for protection.

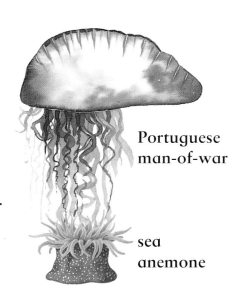

Portuguese man-of-war

sea anemone

△ **Spiny-skinned animals** live on the sea bed. They move around on tube feet, which have suckers on the ends.

▷ **Soft-bodied animals** need to keep their bodies moist, so many of them live in water. Some of them have a hard shell to protect their soft bodies.

snail

octopus

Find out more

Amphibians
Birds
Camouflage
Conservation
Dinosaurs
Fish
Insects
Mammals
Prehistoric life
Reptiles
Spiders
Zoo

Antarctica and Arctic

The Antarctic and Arctic are very cold places. They are found at opposite ends of the Earth. Antarctica is in the south. It is the fifth biggest continent and is completely covered by ice. It is the coldest place on Earth. The Arctic is in the north. Most of it is a frozen ocean. In spring, some of its ice breaks up.

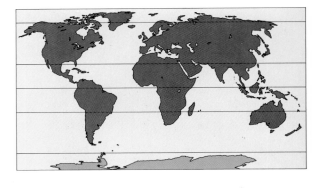

△ The Antarctic is shown in green and the Arctic is right at the top. They are the Earth's coldest places.

▷ Roald Amundsen, a Norwegian explorer, and his team were the first people to reach the South Pole, the centre of the Antarctic.

penguin

▽ Emperor penguins live in Antarctica. They hold their eggs and chicks on their feet to keep them warm.

polar bear

△ Bands of coloured light can be seen in the skies of the Antarctic and Arctic. In the Arctic they are called the northern lights and in the Antarctic, the southern lights.

△ The polar bear lives in the Arctic. It is a strong swimmer and good runner. It catches seals, fish and birds with its strong paws and sharp claws.

△ During the winter in the Arctic and Antarctic it is dark for up to 24 hours a day. In the summer, the opposite happens and the sun shines all night and day.

△ Many scientists work in the Arctic and Antarctic. They record the weather, measure the depth of the ice and study the wildlife.

Find out more
World

21

Ant and Termite

Ants and termites live in enormous nests called colonies. Inside most nests there is a queen who lays eggs, and thousands of workers who run the colony and feed her. Each worker has a job to do – some act as soldiers, guarding the nest, others collect food, and cleaners keep it tidy.

hard outer layer

fungus

chamber

queen

△ In grassland areas, termites build castles of mud that are seven metres tall. Most termites feed on plants, but some live off a fungus that grows in their nests.

▽ A fungus grows in the nests of leafcutter ants. The ants take bits of leaf to the fungus, which 'eats' the leaf and gives off sugars for the ants to eat.

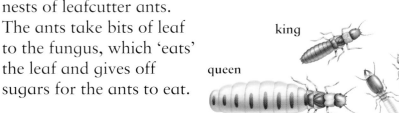

king

queen

worker

soldier

◁ The queen of a termite nest lays 30,000 eggs a day. She can be 11 centimetres long. The king can grow to two centimetres, and the soldiers and workers are about half as big.

▷ Army ants march in vast swarms that can be 12 metres wide. They prey on insects and small animals. The worker ants take the prey back to the nest while the soldier ants stand guard. Termites are sometimes called white ants but termites have softer bodies and wider waists than ants.

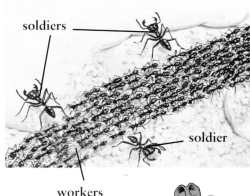

soldiers

soldier

workers

◁ Although not as tall as a termite's nest, there are lots of compartments inside an ant's nest. This is where eggs are laid and where young ants are cared for. Food is stored here too.

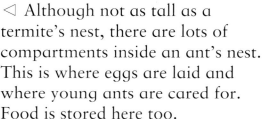

Find out more
Anteater
Bee and Wasp
Insect

Anteater

Anteaters are mammals from South and Central America. As well as eating ants, they feed on termites and other bugs. They may look strange, but their pointy snout, sticky tongue and sharp claws make them perfectly designed for the job of breaking into insect mounds and licking up the tasty creatures inside.

△ The collared anteater catches the termite at home in its nest, high in the trees. Using its long tail to balance itself, the anteater will suck up thousands of termites in just a few minutes.

▷ Giant anteaters shuffle along slowly, carrying their weight on the knuckles of their forefeet to keep their claws sharp for digging. In its first year, a young anteater hitches a ride on its mother's back.

◁ The collared anteater lives in trees in the rainforest. It has a prehensile (gripping) tail. It is one of only two anteaters that live off the ground. They are active at night, sleeping mainly during the day.

Find out more
Ant and Termite
Mammal
Sloth

Antelope

Antelopes graze on the wide plains of Africa and Asia and can run fast. There are many different types of antelope. They range in size from the royal antelope, which is 25 centimetres at the shoulder, to the giant eland, which is 1.75 metres tall. Male antelopes, and sometimes females, have curved horns.

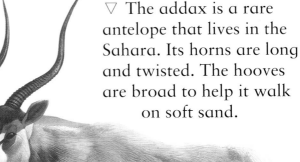

▽ The addax is a rare antelope that lives in the Sahara. Its horns are long and twisted. The hooves are broad to help it walk on soft sand.

◁ Wildebeest, or gnu, are antelopes that migrate in huge herds of up to 500,000. They follow the rain to find rich pastures. Wildebeest are the most common wild grazing animals in East Africa.

▷ Oryx have long, sharp horns and black-and-white faces. They live in the deserts of Arabia and Africa. Two oryx species, the Arabian and the scimitar oryx, have been hunted until there are very few left in the world.

◁ Springboks are small, graceful antelopes that live on the open plains of southern Africa. These animals, which have bold markings, can be 80 centimetres tall. Their name comes from the way they leap, or spring, into the air.

Find out more
Camel
Deer
Llama
Reindeer
Zebra

Arctic tern

Arctic terns make the longest of all animal journeys. In autumn, after nesting on the Arctic coastline, these small sea birds fly south to spend a few months fishing on the other side of the world, in the Antarctic Ocean. In spring, they make the long trip north again to breed.

◁ Arctic terns lay two or three eggs in nests on the frozen Arctic ground, or tundra. They defend their eggs and chicks by diving at attacking predators.

△ The Arctic tern's round trip may be more than 36,000 kilometres. But, by being at each pole in summer, it spends nearly all its life in daylight. Chicks hatch in the northern summer, and by autumn they are ready to make the marathon flight south with their parents.

▽ Sooty and fairy terns are found on tropical islands. Unlike Arctic terns, they do not migrate.

sooty tern

fairy tern

Find out more
Albatross
Gull
Migration
Sea bird

Art and artists

Art is something beautiful made by a person. Painting, carving, pottery and weaving are a few of the different types of art. Artists make works of art for all sorts of reasons. They may want to tell a story or record a place, a person or a special event. Sometimes artists can create things for a magical or religious reason, or just for pleasure.

△ The Aborigines of Australia painted rock or cave pictures thousands of years ago.

◁ The Ancient Greeks painted scenes from everyday life on their pottery vases. This man is hunting deer.

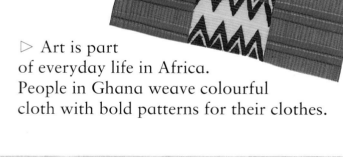

▷ Art is part of everyday life in Africa. People in Ghana weave colourful cloth with bold patterns for their clothes.

▷ This beautiful print of a stormy sea was made by a Japanese artist, called Hokusai. Scenes from nature are popular art subjects in Japan.

▽ This Polynesian sculptor is carving a stone figure called a tiki. He uses a hammer and sharp chisel to carve out the image.

▷ Edgar Degas, a French painter, painted many pictures of ballet dancers. He was interested in movement.

◁ Jackson Pollock, an American artist, laid his canvases on the floor and dripped, threw or poured paint all over them. The paint made swirling shapes and patterns.

Find out more

Africa
Books
Colour
Stories

27

Asia

Asia is the biggest continent. It has many kinds of land. There are large forests, deserts and grasslands. It has many high mountains and some very long rivers. More than half the world's people live in Asia. Many live in large, busy cities. Very few people live in the deserts or the rocky mountain areas.

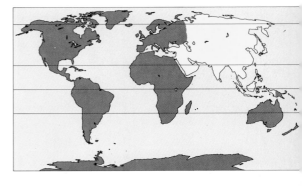

△ Asia is shown in yellow on this map. It covers nearly one third of all the land on the Earth.

▽ Camels are raced in the desert country of Saudi Arabia. Camels carry goods across the desert. They can travel for days without drinking.

△ Rice is grown in the warm, wet parts of Asia. Here it is grown in fields cut into the mountainside. The low-walled fields are flooded with water.

◁ Kyrgyz girls and women wear colourful clothes everyday. Kyrgyzstan is in northern Asia. The people herd sheep in winter and farm in summer.

◁ Shanghai, in China, is a very busy, crowded city. It is also the biggest city in China. New skyscrapers are being built to provide homes.

△ The tea ceremony is a very old and popular ceremony in Japan. The tea is made and drunk very slowly and carefully.

◁ The highest mountains in the world are in the Himalayas, between India and China. The highest of all is Mount Everest.

▽ Every July, at full moon, richly decorated elephants parade with dancers and drummers through the streets of Kandy in Sri Lanka.

Find out more

Dance
Drama
Farming
Religion
World

Australia and the Pacific Islands

Australia is the smallest continent and it is also a country. It is hot. Most people live in cities on the coast. Away from the coasts the land is called the bush and the outback. The Pacific is the world's largest and deepest ocean. It has many small islands. The Pacific islands, Australia and New Zealand together make up Oceania.

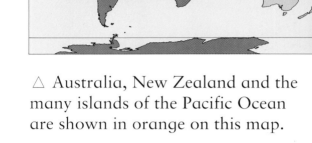

△ Australia, New Zealand and the many islands of the Pacific Ocean are shown in orange on this map.

△ A sheep shearer clips off a sheep's wool. Huge sheep stations cover large parts of Australia and New Zealand.

▽ Many Pacific islands are surrounded by coral reefs. Many kinds of brightly coloured fish live in the warm waters of the reef.

▷ These didgeridoo-players are Aborigines. Their ancestors were the first people to settle in Australia, a long time ago.

▷ Sydney is the largest city in Australia. It is also Australia's oldest city. Its world-famous Opera House (on the left of this picture) overlooks the harbour.

Uluru (Ayers Rock)

▷ The koala lives among the branches of eucalyptus trees. It feeds at night and sleeps all day. Its strong claws and special fingers help it cling to tree trunks.

koala bear

▽ On the North Island of New Zealand there are many geysers, which are jets of boiling water that burst into the air.

Find out more
Buildings
Farming
History
Stories
World

Babies

Very young children are called babies. A baby begins when a tiny egg inside its mother joins together with a tiny part of its father called a sperm. The baby grows inside its mother's womb where it is kept safe and warm. After about nine months, the baby is ready to be born.

sperm —

egg

◁ This egg is surrounded by lots of sperm. Only one of the sperm will get inside the egg.

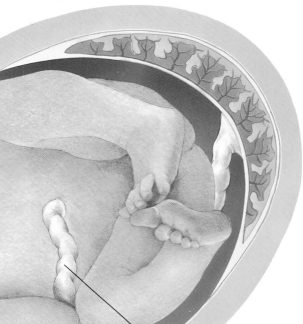

▷ A baby grows inside its mother's womb. It gets all the food it needs through a tube called the umbilical cord.

umbilical cord

▽ A new born baby needs a lot of care and attention. It must be fed, bathed, kept warm and protected.

▷ Most babies start to walk without help between the ages of 12 and 18 months.

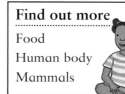

Find out more
Food
Human body
Mammals

Baboon

Baboons are large monkeys that live in troops of over 100 in number. They feed on many different foods, from seeds, fruits and grasses to small animals and eggs. They are found in Arabia and in Africa, south of the Sahara.

△ Baboons spend much of their time grooming each other. This helps form bonds between babies and mothers, and also between members of the troop. The troop is usually made up of related females, males and one lead male.

▽ Mandrills, from the West African rainforests, are cousins of the baboon. They have bare patches on their large faces. In adult males, these are brightly coloured.

▷ The gelada is a monkey similar to a baboon found in the mountains of Ethiopia, in East Africa. It has a hairless red patch in the centre of its chest, from which it gets its other name – the 'bleeding heart baboon'. The males have very long hair over their head and shoulders.

Fact box
• Baboons sometimes weigh 40kg. They can be 1.15m long, and have tails of 70cm.
• Male baboons are twice as big as females.
• Baboons bark like dogs when frightened.

Find out more
Chimpanzee
Gorilla
Monkey
Orang-utan

Baby animal

When they are young, many animals need looking after, just as human babies do. Their parents must keep them safe from harm and find food for them until they are old enough to look after themselves.

△ When danger threatens, the male mouthbreeder fish shelters his young in his mouth. He spits them out as soon as it is safe.

△ The merganser duck sometimes gives its babies a piggyback. This keeps them safe until they are old enough to swim by themselves.

△ A zebra foal must learn to walk straight after it is born so it can follow its mother away from danger. The male zebras will protect the herd by kicking and biting any attackers.

△ Emperor penguins keep their babies warm by carrying them on their feet.

◁ Play the baby penguin game with four or more people. Divide into two teams and stand in rows. The aim is to pass a bean-bag along each row using only your feet. The first team to get the bean-bag along the row wins.

Find out more

Alligator and Crocodile

Gorilla

Mammal

Penguin

Reptile

Badger

Badgers are powerful creatures, but they are also shy. They are related to skunks and, like them, have black and white markings. In Europe, they live in family groups in woodlands.

▽ Badgers are omnivores, which means that they eat all kinds of food. Their diet includes grasses, fruit and nuts, as well as small animals and eggs. They are good at digging and often catch earthworms.

▽ Badgers are most active in the evening. This is when they come out to feed and to collect straw for bedding.

◁ During the day, badgers stay in burrows called setts. As the group of badgers grows bigger, they dig more underground chambers. Some large setts have been used for hundreds of years.

▷ Unlike the European badger, the American badger lives alone for most of the year in dry, open countryside. It also has a different face pattern.

Find out more
Mole
Skunk

Bat

Bats have big ears, furry bodies and wings like leather. They are nocturnal mammals. This means they sleep in caves and attics during the day and fly out to feed at night-time.

▽ Bats are the only mammals that can fly. They are very fast and acrobatic. When they chase after insects, they twist and turn in mid-air.

△ Bats use sound to catch insects in the darkness. They send out high-pitched squeals that humans cannot hear. The echoes that bounce back tell the bats exactly where they will find their prey.

Fact box
• The 'bumblebee', or hog-nosed bat may be the world's smallest mammal. It is only two centimetres long.
• The South American vampire bat feeds on the blood of living animals.

▷ Flying foxes, or fruit bats, are large bats that live in tropical Africa and Asia. They mainly eat fruit. Flying foxes are important because they help to spread the pollen and seeds of many plants.

Find out more
Bird
Insect
Mouse

Battery

A battery is a source of electricity. The electricity is made inside the battery by chemicals. When you turn on a torch, electricity flows along a wire from one end of the battery, through a bulb and back to the battery to make the torch glow. After a while, the chemicals are used up and can no longer produce electricity. Then we say that the battery has run down or is flat.

△ All the machines above use batteries to work. Because the batteries inside them are small, the machines are light and portable. This makes them easy to carry around.

▽ This battery is rechargeable. This means that when it runs down the chemicals can be replaced by sending electricity through it. Most cars have battery like this to start their engines.

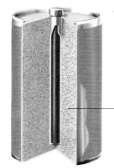

chemical paste

△ This is the type of battery used in a torch or a radio. It is called a dry battery, because the chemicals inside it are like a dry paste.

Never play with batteries or take them apart. They can be dangerous.

▷ This car has an electric motor instead of a petrol engine. The electricity for the motor comes from rechargeable batteries inside the car.

Find out more
Chemistry and Chemicals
Electricity

Bear

The bear is the largest meat-eating animal on Earth. There are many kinds of bear and most of them live in northern parts of the world. Their thick fur coats protect them from the cold.

Kodiak bear

brown bear

polar bear

black bear

△ Most bears are large and powerful, with strong claws and a good sense of smell. The Kodiak bear of Alaska is the largest of all. It weighs almost 800 kilograms and, when standing up, can be four metres tall.

◁ In winter, some bears find a snug place to hibernate.
   Hibernation is a very deep sleep that may last many weeks. The workings of the bear's body slow down to save energy.

◁ In the autumn, American black bears hunt salmon and eat berries and honey. This helps them to put on the weight they need in order to survive their long hibernation.

Find out more
Mammal
Polar bear
Raccoon

Beaver

Beavers live near rivers in North America and northern Europe. They are great builders and use their massive front teeth to cut down trees. Beavers use these trees to make their homes, which are called lodges.

Fact box

• Beaver dams can be over 500m long and up to 4m high.
• Some beaver dams are 1,000 years old.
• A male and female pair of beavers will stay together for their whole lives.

△ Beavers dam the river with branches to make a pond. In this pond they will build their lodge. Beavers use their webbed feet and big flat tails to push themselves through the water. If alarmed, they slap their tails on the water to warn other beavers.

◁ Beaver lodges are made of sticks and mud. Beavers seal their lodges with more mud during the winter. The mud freezes hard and helps to keep out predators.

▽ The adults enter the lodge by an underwater entrance and bring food to their young hidden inside. The young beavers will stay with their family for about two years. Then they leave to build their own lodges.

dam

lodge

Find out more

Mouse
Otter
Rabbit and Hare
Rat

Bee and Wasp

Bees and wasps are easy insects to spot because of their black and yellow, or black and white, striped bodies. Wasps and worker bees have a stinging tail. Bees only sting in self-defence and usually die afterwards.

▽ Honeybees are ruled by a queen. They build wax rooms, called cells. **1** The queen lays an egg in each cell. **2** This grows into a larva. **3, 4** The worker bees feed it. **5, 6** Soon it grows into an adult and emerges.

△ Bees collect the sweet juice, or nectar, from flowers and use it to make honey. They keep the honey in cells to feed their growing young.

◁ The bumblebee is larger and more furry than the honeybee. It collects pollen from flowers using its hindlegs. Flowers need bees to spread pollen from one flower to another. This way, the flowers can reproduce.

1

2

3

4

5

6

▽ Wasps are different from bees because they feed their young on insects, not honey. They use their sting to kill the insects. Adult wasps eat the sugars found in fruit, and so are attracted by the smell of sweet food or liquids.

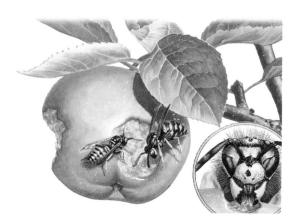

Find out more
Ant and Termite
Fly
Insect

Beetle

There are over a quarter of a million species of beetle in the world. They come in many shapes and sizes, but all have one thing in common – a pair of delicate, folded wings protected by a hard outer casing or shell.

△ Some species of water beetle hunt tadpoles and baby fish. Before diving, the beetles come to the surface to collect air under their wing casings.

◁ Fireflies are not flies, but flying beetles that glow in the dark. They give off light from their abdomen (rear body part) to attract mates. They let out short, regular flashes – each species has its own typical flash pattern. In some of the 1,900 species the female does not fly. She is called a glow-worm.

△ Dung beetles collect a ball of dung and lay an egg in it. When the egg hatches, the new beetle larva eats the dung.

▽ Stag beetles are huge, measuring up to 7.5 centimetres long. The males often fight each other with their large jaws.

Find out more
Ant and Termite
Dragonfly and Damselfly
Fly
Insect

Bikes

Bicycles, or bikes, are two-wheeled machines used to travel around. On a bike you can go from place to place much faster than you can walk. Motorbikes have engines and they can travel as fast as cars. Pedal bikes are a cheap, quiet and clean way to get around.

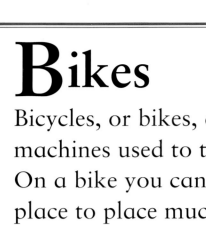

◁ This wooden bike was built over a hundred years ago.

handlebar

saddle

fuel tank

exhaust pipe

engine

△ The engine of a motorbike makes the wheels go round. The engine runs on petrol, which is stored in the fuel tank.

▽ To ride a bike you push the pedals. The pedals turn the chain. The chain moves the back wheel round. This makes the bike move.

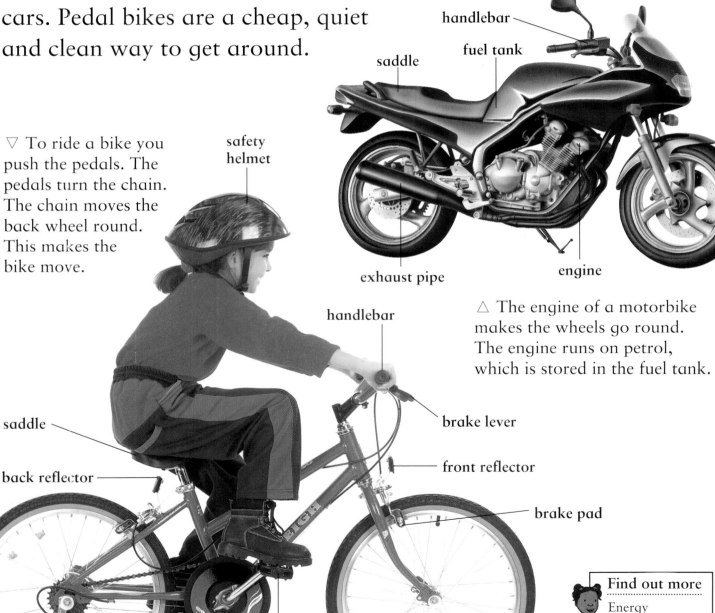

safety helmet

handlebar

brake lever

front reflector

brake pad

saddle

back reflector

pedal

chain

Find out more
Energy
Inventions
Machines

Biology

How does your body work? Why are leaves green? Biology is the study of living things, so it can help answer questions like these. It tells us how animals and plants live, grow, produce young and find food.

Doctors use biology to find out about illnesses and medicines. Scientists who study biology are called biologists.

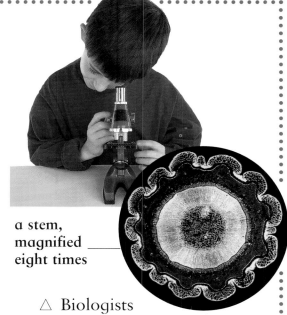

a stem, magnified eight times

△ Biologists often use a microscope to study tiny objects, such as the cells inside plant stems. Try looking at animal hairs or a leaf under a microscope.

△ Like other scientists, biologists often work in laboratories. This biologist is studying some specially grown seedlings.

▽ Biologists often choose to study just one kind of living thing. Some biologists study mostly plants, others study mostly animals. They may make trips to other parts of the world, like this tropical rainforest, to study the plants or animals that live there.

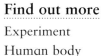

Find out more
Experiment
Human body
Living things
Medicine

Birds

Birds are the only animals with feathers. They also have wings. There are thousands of different birds, of all shapes, sizes and colours. The biggest bird in the world is an ostrich. The smallest bird is the tiny bee hummingbird, which is about the size of an ostrich's eye.

tail feathers

eye

ear

beak

claw

wing

▷ Many male birds have colourful feathers to attract a female bird. A peacock shows off to a peahen.

peacock

▽ An ostrich has wings, but it is too heavy to fly. It uses its strong legs to run quickly. An ostrich can run faster than a racehorse.

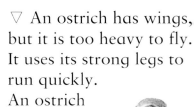

▽ Most birds build nests for their eggs. When the chicks hatch the adult birds feed them. They are fed until they can leave the nest to find food.

herring gull

ostrich

wren

avocet

toucan

▷ A wren's beak is shaped for snapping up insects. An avocet has a long, curved beak to scoop up small water animals. A toucan uses its big beak to push aside leaves to pick fruit and nuts.

▽ Some birds are hunters. The powerful eagle uses its sharp, hooked talons to catch its prey.

eagle

talon

Fact box

• Birds have beaks, or bills, instead of teeth.

• All birds hatch from eggs. The eggs have hard shells and are laid by the female bird.

• Most birds can fly. Penguins are birds that cannot fly. They use their wings to swim.

• Many birds have some hollow bones that help to make them light enough to fly.

Canada geese

▷ In autumn, many birds migrate. This means they fly away to warmer places where they can find food more easily.

embryo

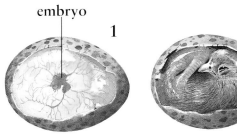

1   2

chick

3

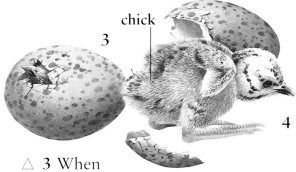

4

△ 1 Each bird's egg has an embryo. This is the part that can grow into a chick. 2 The chick grows bigger and bigger.

△ 3 When the chick is ready to hatch, it chips a hole in the eggshell. 4 Then the chick breaks out of the shell.

Find out more
Air
Animals
Antarctica and Arctic
Conservation
Prehistoric life
Seashore

Books

scrolls

The first books were rare and precious. They were written by hand, which took a long time. Then a machine called a printing press was invented. This made it possible to make many copies of each book. Today most books are made of paper and cardboard. They are printed in enormous numbers on fast machines.

◁ The Ancient Egyptians made some of the first books. They were written on scrolls.

▷ Long ago monks copied books by hand. They decorated each page with patterns and pictures.

▽ This printing machine was built by Johannes Gutenberg, over 500 years ago. The Bible was one of the first books he printed.

How a book is made

△ A team of people meet to plan the book. They decide on its size and what it will look like. They also choose an author to write it.

△ When the author has written the words, an editor carefully reads them. The editor corrects any mistakes on a computer screen.

△ An illustrator draws pictures to go with the words. Sometimes a photographer takes photographs to put in the book too.

△ The designer decides how to arrange the words and pictures on each page. She then puts the pages on to a computer disk.

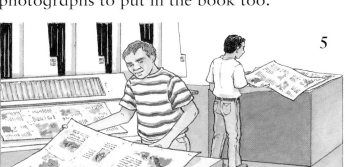

△ From the disk, film and printing plates are made. At the printers a printing press prints the pages on to large sheets of paper.

△ The printed sheets are folded and cut into separate pages. They are stitched or glued together. Then a cover is put around the pages.

▷ You can use books to find out facts about animals, machines, history or science. Other books have stories in them. Millions of books are made every year.

Find out more
Forests
History
Stories

Buildings

Buildings give us shelter in all sorts of weather. Houses are often made of whatever materials can be found easily and most cheaply. They are built in all sorts of sizes and styles. Some buildings are built for a special purpose, such as offices, factories, sports centres and cinemas. Can you think of any others?

△ Log cabins were often built near forests. They had stone chimneys to protect the house from the fire.

△ Stone is very heavy. Stone houses were usually built in areas where the stone could be found nearby.

▽ Bundles of woven reeds are used to build houses in the marshes of Iraq in the Middle East. The houses are built on islands.

▽ In hot places, such as Africa, buildings are sometimes made of mud, baked by the sun. These are cool and shady.

△ Many houses are made of bricks. The bricks are joined with mortar, a mixture of water, sand and cement.

Famous Buildings

Leaning
Tower of
Pisa

Sydney Opera House

◁ Sydney Opera
House, Australia
overlooks a large
harbour. Its roof
looks like the sails
of a boat.

◁ Italy's Leaning
Tower of Pisa was
built on soft ground.
Every year the tower
leans a tiny bit more.

▷ The Epcot Center
at Disney World
in Florida, USA,
looks like a giant
golf ball.

Epcot
Centre

◁ Skyscrapers
have a skeleton
made of steel.
The walls are
made of glass
panels and thin
concrete sheets.

Find out more

Australia and
the Pacific
Islands
Castles
Religion
Sport

Butterfly and Moth

These flying insects are found worldwide, especially in warm places. Most butterflies are colourful and fly by day. Moths fly at night and are usually dull in colouring.

△ Swallowtail butterflies are so-called because their wings look like the tails of swallows.

1 egg

2 caterpillar

3 pupa

4 adult

△ **1** The female butterfly lays her eggs on a branch and these hatch into caterpillars. **2, 3** The caterpillar eats the leaves and grows fast, until it is ready to spin itself a hard case, called a pupa. **4** Over time, it starts to change and soon becomes an adult butterfly.

▽ The death's head hawk moth of Africa gets its name from the skull-shaped pattern on its back.

◁ See for yourself how caterpillars turn into butterflies. Collect some caterpillars and put them in a large jar, along with the branches you found them on. Fasten some net across the top with an elastic band. Add fresh leaves every day and watch the changes as they happen. Make sure you let the butterflies go as soon as they can fly.

Find out more
Bee and Wasp
Cricket and Grasshopper
Insect
Reproduction

Calculator

A calculator is a machine that adds, subtracts, multiplies and divides. We often use electronic calculators. These can help us work out difficult sums quickly and without making mistakes.

▽ This calculator is called an abacus. The different beads stand for different numbers. You do the sums by sliding the beads along the wires. Calculators like this have been used for over 5,000 years.

▽ The display window on a calculator shows each stage of a calculation while you are doing it. When you have finished the calculation, the answer appears in the window.

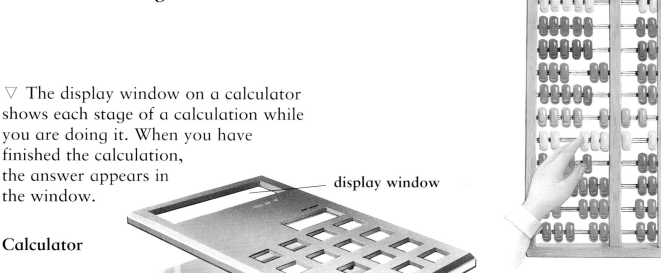

Calculator

display window

keypad

electronic circuits

battery

◁ You press the buttons on the keypad to enter the sum into the calculator.

◁ This calculator has a small battery inside it that makes the electricity it needs to work.

◁ Inside every calculator is a tiny microchip like this one. It contains very complicated electrical circuits. When electricity passes through these, they do the calculations.

Find out more
Battery
Computers
Electricity
Mathematics
Numbers

Camel

Camels live in the world's driest deserts. They have humps of fat on their backs that help them survive for days without food or water.

Fact box

- Camels can go without water for up to 17 days.
- Camels can drink 100 litres of water at a go.
- Because they carry people and cargo across the sandy wastes, camels are known as 'ships of the desert'.

▽ A camel's feet are big and wide to stop it from sinking into the desert sand.

△ Camels have been used since ancient times to carry people across deserts.

△ A camel has two rows of eyelashes to shield its eyes in a sandstorm. It can also close its nostrils tight.

◁ The Arabian camel, or dromedary, has one hump. The Bactrian camel has two humps. Bactrians live in Central Asia; dromedaries live in North Africa, the Middle East and India.

Find out more

Antelope
Cow and Ox
Giraffe
Llama

Camera

A camera is a machine for taking photographs. When you take a photograph of an object, light bounces off it and in through the camera's lens to hit the film inside. The light changes chemicals in the film. When the film is processed (treated with more chemicals), the pictures appear.

1

△ **1** Try making this simple camera, which is called a pin-hole camera. You need a small box. Cut off its ends and colour the inside with a black marker pen.

2

△ **2** Cover one end with tracing paper. Cover the other end with brown paper and pierce a small hole in its centre.

▽ **3** Point your camera at a window or a light so that light streams through the pin-hole. Can you see an upside-down image on the tracing paper? You will see the image better if you cut out stray light by putting a towel over your head as in the picture above.

3

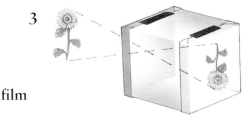

Camera

shutter release button

viewfinder (you look through this)

film   shutter

lens

film

◁ Here you can see the parts of a compact camera. Behind the lens there is a shutter, which opens and shuts very fast. It lets just enough light into the camera for a picture to form on the film.

Find out more
Chemistry and Chemicals
Colour
Light and Lenses

Camouflage

Many animals use camouflage – body shapes, colours or markings that make them blend in with their background. Camouflage helps animals hide when hunting or being hunted.

△ The tiger's stripes help it blend in with the tall grass on the sunny, open plain where it lives. This makes the tiger hard to spot as it waits to ambush its prey.

◁ The plaice hides by lying flat on the seabed and changing colour to match the sand and pebbles.

▷ Leaf insects look almost the same as a leaf. They also move slowly to try to fool predators into thinking they are leaves. Even their eggs are leaf-shaped.

△ **1** Play a camouflage game with some friends. First you need to find three or four everyday objects, such as a tin, a bottle and a carton. Then stick leaves, grass and scraps of paper to them. Finally, paint them with brown or green paint.

▷ **2** Take the objects into the garden and put them amongst the plants. Tell your friends what you have hidden and challenge them to find the objects. The person who finds the most things wins.

Find out more

Chameleon
Evolution
Tiger
Zebra

Cars

People drive all kinds of cars. There are family cars, racing cars, police cars, taxis, cross-country cars and long cars, called stretch-limousines. Most cars are powered by engines that need fuel to make the go. A few cars run on gas or electricity. Some even use energy from sunlight.

△ The first petrol-driven car was invented by a German, Karl Benz. He put an engine into a horse cart.

windscreen

engine

petrol tank

axle

Formula 1 racing car

▽ A racing car can go faster than other cars because of its powerful engine and wide wheels.

△ A car has hundreds of different moving parts to make it go.

Jeep

▷A Jeep is specially built to be driven over very bumpy ground. It also travels easily across deep mud and ice.

Find out more
Computers
Conservation
Energy
Inventions
Machines
Roads

Castles

Most castles were built hundreds of years ago. They had high towers and thick walls that sheltered people from their enemies. The first castles were built of wood. Later they were built of stone. Castles often have deep ditches around them called moats.

motte

bailey

△ Wooden castles were built on a mound called a motte. People lived in an area outside the castle called a bailey. They only went into the castle when they were attacked.

▽ Armies attacked big castles. They used tall wooden towers, huge catapults and battering rams to try to break into the castle.

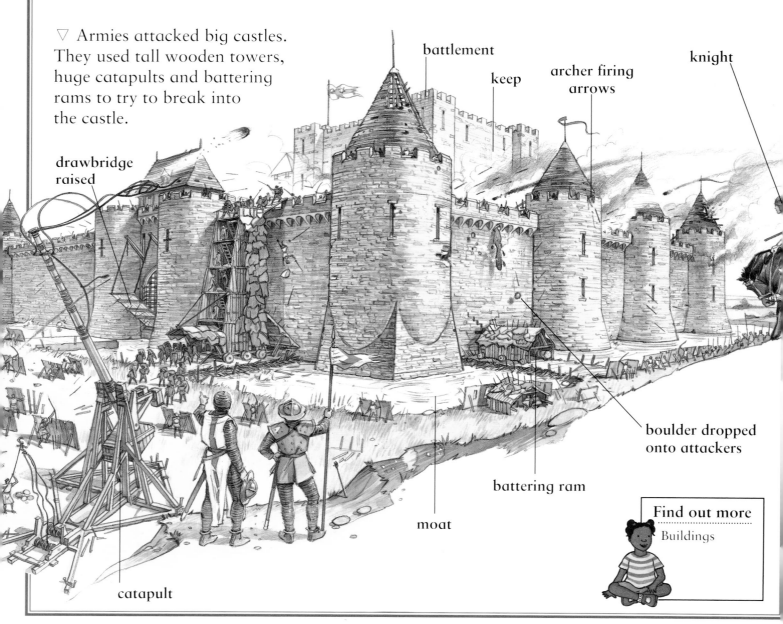

battlement

keep

archer firing arrows

knight

drawbridge raised

boulder dropped onto attackers

battering ram

moat

catapult

Find out more
Buildings

Cat (domestic)

All the domestic or house cats of today are descended from wild cats. They were first tamed over 4,000 years ago in ancient Egypt. Although domestic cats are fed by humans, they are still hunters like their ancestors, and have the same sharp teeth, pointed claws and sensitive eyes for seeing in the dark.

tortoiseshell

blue tabby

chocolate point Siamese

▷ There are now over 40 different 'breeds' of cat. Some, like the Siamese, have short hair. Others, like Persian cats, are long haired.

◁ Cats make good pets, as they are clean, quiet and friendly. They can be quite independent but still need to be well cared for. Kittens have to be trained so that they become used to humans and learn good habits in the home. They enjoy human contact, especially being stroked.

▷ The African wildcat is probably the domestic cat's main ancestor, although other cats have also been taken from the wild and tamed by humans. African wildcats look like domestic tabbies, but they are slightly bigger. Their fur is also thicker and the markings are not as bold.

African wildcat

domestic cat

Find out more
Cat (wild)
Cheetah
Lion
Mammal

Cat (wild)

Apart from the big cats like lions and tigers, most wild members of the cat family are fairly small. Many wild cats are hunted for their boldly patterned coats. Because of this, some are in real danger of extinction and need protection in the wild.

▽ Caracals are cats that live in dry, scrubby areas of India and Africa. They particularly like to eat birds and will often leap up to catch them. The saying 'Putting the cat among the pigeons' comes from the actions of this cat.

△ The European wildcat is found in forests from western Asia, through the continent of Europe, to Scotland. They are nocturnal animals that hunt birds and small mammals for food. The female gives birth to between three and six kittens.

Fact box
• The smallest cat is the rusty-spotted cat, at just 35 centimetres long. It lives in India.
• The fishing cat of India has webbed paws.
• European wildcats can be 40 centimetres at the shoulder and weigh up to ten kilograms.

△ The North American bobcat gets its name from its short (bobbed) tail. It lives in forests and deserts and catches rabbits, mice and squirrels.

Find out more
Cat (domestic)
Lion
Tiger

Caves

Caves are big holes in rock. They are usually underground and are dark and damp. Most underground caves are found in rock called limestone. Rainwater and rivers can eat away limestone rocks. Sea water also crashes on to cliffs and hollows out caves. Caves can be used for shelter too.

bats

△ Bats often live in caves. They sleep in them during the day and fly out to hunt after dark. The caves are a safe place for their young.

△ Water sinks into the cracks in limestone. It eats away at the rock to make tunnels.

△ Over thousands of years the tunnels get deeper and wider until they make big caves.

stalactite

pillar

stalagmite

▷ Water dripping from the cave roof has minerals in it. When the water dries the minerals are left behind. They make stalactites, stalagmites and pillars.

Find out more

Art

Water

59

Centipede

Many animals are so small that they can only be seen under a magnifying glass. We call these animals minibeasts. Minibeasts are invertebrates, which means that they have no backbone.

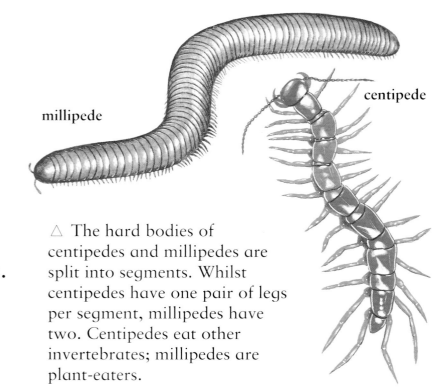
millipede
centipede

△ The hard bodies of centipedes and millipedes are split into segments. Whilst centipedes have one pair of legs per segment, millipedes have two. Centipedes eat other invertebrates; millipedes are plant-eaters.

◁ There are many types of minibeast. Spiders are arachnids, and they have eight legs.

▷ Woodlice are land-living crustaceans, a group normally found in water.

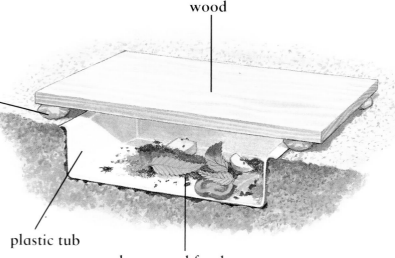
wood
stone
plastic tub
leaves and food scraps

◁ Wasps are insects. They have six legs, and bodies with three sections.

▷ Snails are molluscs that carry their shells on their backs.

△ A good way of catching minibeasts is by making a trap. Put a plastic container in a hole and add some leaves, twigs and scraps of food. Cover it with a piece of wood supported on stones. Leave your trap overnight. How many types of minibeast did you catch?

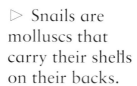

◁ Worms belong to a group called the annelids. They have long, soft bodies that are divided into many segments.

Find out more
Bee and Wasp
Insect
Slug and Snail
Spider

Chameleon

Chameleons are unusual lizards that can change their skin colour. They do this when they are angry or frightened, when the light or temperature levels change, or to hide themselves.

△ There are special cells called melanophores underneath a chameleon's skin. These can change colour to match the chameleon's surroundings, making it more difficult to see.

▽ A chameleon will sit in a tree waiting to catch insects. A strong, curled tail holds it to the branch, while swivelling eyes allow it to see prey in two directions at the same time. Then its long tongue darts out to catch the prey.

Fact box

• There are about 100 species of chameleon.
• Around 50 of these species live on the island of Madagascar.
• Most chameleons live in trees, but come down to lay their eggs in the soil.

▷ The Madagascan pygmy chameleon is the smallest species at about 2.5 centimetres long. It lives mainly on leaves on the forest floor. Most chameleons are between 17 and 25 centimetres long, but some can grow up to 60 centimetres. While most chameleons eat insects, the bigger ones also eat birds.

Find out more
Alligator and Crocodile
Cobra
Lizard
Reptile

Cheetah

Cheetahs are slim, spotted cats with long legs. They are the fastest land animals and can reach speeds of over 100 kilometres per hour. Cheetahs are found in the open plains of Africa, south of the Sahara.

△ Cheetahs can only run at high speed for a short distance They bring down their prey by tripping them up.

◁ Female cheetahs have up to four babies at a time. The cubs have a long coat of grey hair, which makes them look like honey badgers. Honey badgers are aggressive animals so other animals will not go near them. This 'disguise' keeps the cubs safe from harm.

Fact box
• Cheetahs are the only cats that cannot draw their claws back fully. They use them to grip while sprinting after prey.
• Cheetahs are 1.4m long and have tails measuring 80cm.

▷ Cheetahs once lived in North Africa, the Middle East and India. But they have been trapped and tamed in Asia, and are now seriously endangered. Cheetahs are also rare in Africa.

Find out more
Cat (wild)
Lion
Tiger

Chemistry and Chemicals

Chemistry is the study of what things are made from. People who study chemistry are called chemists. Chemicals are the solids, liquids and gases that chemists use or make.

Different chemicals are useful in different ways. We use some for cleaning and others for cooking. Some are used in factories, to make plastics or paint. Farmers use chemicals to help crops to grow, and to kill weeds or insects.

carbon
atom

hydrogen
atom

△ Like all substances, chemicals are made up of atoms. These cling together in groups called molecules. This picture shows a model of a polythene molecule. It is made up of carbon and hydrogen atoms.

▷ Some chemicals seem to disappear when you put them in water. We say they dissolve. How well do salt, sugar and flour dissolve?

sugar

salt

flour

sugar

salt

△ Sugar and salt are chemicals that look the same. Is it easy to tell them apart by tasting them?

oil

▽ Some chemicals look the same, but you can tell them apart by feeling them. Try touching lemon juice and cooking oil.

Don't touch any chemicals unless an adult says they are safe. Some are poisonous. Some can burn your skin.

lemon juice

▽ Rust is made when the metal iron combines with the gas oxygen (which is in the air). When chemicals join together to make new chemicals, we call it a chemical reaction.

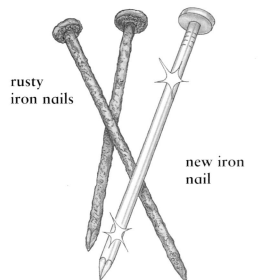

rusty iron nails

new iron nail

△ Hundreds of years ago, people called alchemists tried to make gold from other kinds of metals. This was impossible but, as they worked, alchemists learned about what happened when they mixed different chemicals. In a way, alchemists were the first chemists.

▷ We can tell some chemicals by their smell. Slices of potato and apple look the same but smell different.

potato

pebble

polystyrene pebble

apple

Fact box

• Chemicals can occur in very different forms. For example, graphite (found in pencils) and diamonds are both forms of the chemical carbon.

△ We can tell some chemicals apart by their weight. For example, a lump of polystyrene weighs much less than a rock the same size.

Find out more

Acid
Fuels
Gases
Solids

Chicken and Turkey

Chickens and turkeys are kept as farm animals all over the world. They are related to wild birds that were tamed by humans over 4,000 years ago. Chickens and turkeys can fly for short distances, but they prefer to walk or run.

△ Farmyard chickens eat seeds and small insects. They will also peck grain that is sprinkled on the ground. On some big farms, however, hens are fed on special food and kept in small cages.

△ Male chickens are called cockerels and have large crests on their heads and a ruff of long feathers round their necks. They often make a loud crow, especially at daybreak. Female chickens are called hens. They are smaller and less colourful than cockerels. Hens are kept for both their meat and their eggs.

◁ Turkeys are big birds with a fleshy red 'wattle' round their necks. They come from North and Central America, and were first brought to Europe in about 1519 by Spanish explorers.

Find out more
Bird
Duck and Goose
Peacock
Swan

Chimpanzee

Chimpanzees, or chimps, are our closest animal relatives, and are some of the most intelligent animals. They live in tropical rainforests and woodlands in Africa. Chimps eat fruits, leaves and seeds, but they also like termites and ants.

△ Chimps sometimes use twigs to prise insects out of their mounds, and will crack nuts open by hitting them with stones.

Fact box
- The tallest male chimps are about 1.6m tall when they stand up – almost as big as a small human adult. Female chimps are shorter.
- Chimps can live to be 60 years old.
- Chimps live in groups. These have between 15 and 80 members.

△ Chimps spend a lot of their time in trees. They use their long arms to swing from branch to branch in search of food. At night, they build nests of leaves to sleep in.

◁ Chimps usually move about on all fours, but they can also walk upright, which leaves their hands free. If attacked, a chimp may defend itself by throwing stones.

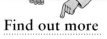

Find out more
Baboon
Gorilla
Monkey
Orang-utan

Clocks

We use clocks to measure time. Inside every clock there is a special part that works at the same, regular speed. In electric clocks it is a regular electrical signal. This controls the speed at which the hands move, or how often the numbers on the display change. Some older clocks have a swinging pendulum to move the hands at a regular speed.

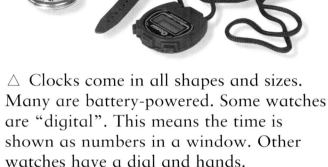

△ Clocks come in all shapes and sizes. Many are battery-powered. Some watches are "digital". This means the time is shown as numbers in a window. Other watches have a dial and hands.

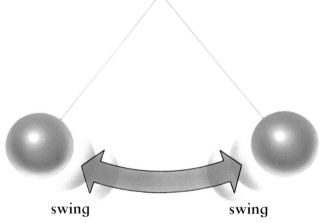

swing   swing

△ A pendulum is a weight on the end of a string or rod. Each swing of the pendulum takes exactly the same time.

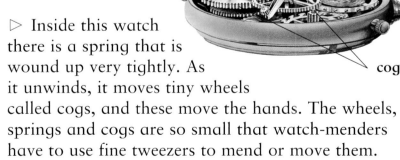

tweezers

cogs

▷ Inside this watch there is a spring that is wound up very tightly. As it unwinds, it moves tiny wheels called cogs, and these move the hands. The wheels, springs and cogs are so small that watch-menders have to use fine tweezers to mend or move them.

◁ This old-fashioned grandfather clock has a long pendulum to control the speed of its hands.

◁ Long ago, people used sundials instead of clocks. The dial is marked in hours. The Sun shines on the pointer, which casts a shadow. This shows you the time.

Find out more
Day and Night
Energy
Machines

Clothes

All the things we wear are called clothes. People wear different clothes to suit the jobs they do, the games they play and the weather. In some jobs people wear uniforms so that they are easy to recognise. Most of the clothes we wear are made in factories.

Inuit child

◁ People that live in very cold places wear clothes that will keep them warm and dry.

Tuareg man

▷ In hot, dry deserts people wear long robes and scarves. They protect them from the heat of the Sun.

▽ When the weather is wet and rainy, you wear waterproof things to keep your clothes dry.

▽ Fire-fighters wear special clothes to protect them from the heat and the smoke.

speed skater

◁ Clothes for sport are often tight and stretchy. They must be light and easy to move in.

fire-fighter

Find out more

Dance
Desert
Drama
Space
exploration
Sports

Cobra

Cobras are poisonous snakes found in Africa, India and Asia. The most deadly cobras are the mambas of Africa. A bite from a mamba will kill unless the victim is given antivenin (an antidote to snake venom) very quickly. Many people die each year from cobra bites.

Fact box

• Cobras eat small vertebrates (creatures with backbones).
• The black mamba moves as fast as a running human.
• Cobra venom stops the heart and lungs from working.

△ The king cobra is found in areas stretching from southern China to Indonesia. Reaching 5.5 metres in length, it is the world's longest poisonous snake. The female king cobra lays up to 40 eggs.

▷ In India, snake charmers catch common cobras. They play a tune on a pipe and the cobra rises up from the basket to 'dance'.

▽ One of the cobra's main predators is the mongoose. Mongooses move very quickly and can avoid getting bitten. When frightened, the cobra rears up and spreads its hood.

Find out more
Lizard
Rattlesnake
Reptile

Colour

When we see colour, we see coloured light. Ordinary light, such as sunlight, is called white light. It seems to have no colour but it is really a mixture of every colour there is.

When we see an object, what we actually see is light bouncing off it into our eyes. Often, only a few of the colours in the light bounce off the object. A leaf looks green, for example, because only green light bounces off it.

Fact box
• The pictures in this book are made up of tiny coloured dots. The colours are yellow, a kind of dark pink, a shade of blue and black. These four colours mix together to make all the colours you see.

1

△ **1** Put a saucer on a sheet of white card. Draw around it and cut out the circle.

2

△ **2** Draw lines to divide the circle into three. Colour one part red, one part green and one part blue.

3

△ **3** Push a pencil through the centre of the circle. Spin it like a top. The three colours mix together, making the disc look white.

△ A rainbow happens when the Sun shines during a shower of rain. The light reflects (bounces off) the raindrops and the light breaks up into all its different colours.

▽ Red, blue and green are called the primary colours of light because they mix together to make white light.

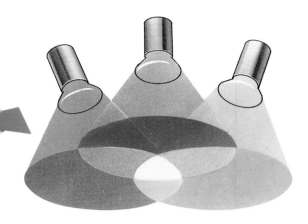

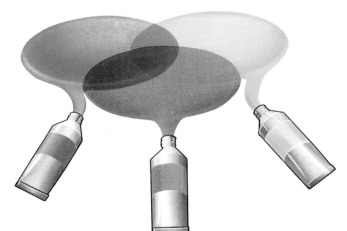

△ Red, blue and yellow are the primary colours of paint. With these three colours you can make any colour you want.

△ Flowers are often brightly coloured. Their colours signal to insects and birds that there is sweet nectar inside, which they like to drink. This hummingbird uses its long, thin beak to reach deep inside the flower.

▽ The ladybird's colouring warns other animals that it is not good to eat.

▷ We use coloured lights to send messages. On traffic lights, red means "stop", amber means "take care" and green means "go".

◁ This insect is exactly the same colour as the leaves it lives on. Its disguise makes it difficult for its enemies to see and protects the insect from being eaten.

Find out more
Light and Lenses
Living things

Computers

A computer is an amazing machine. It can do calculations, store and find information. It works using microchips (very small electrical circuits), which act as its brain and memory. A computer cannot think for itself. A human being has to give it a set of instructions, called a program. These are usually stored on a disk inside the computer.

△ A CD-ROM is a disk containing information that the computer can turn into words, pictures and sounds.

▷ The letters and pictures that appear on a computer screen are made of tiny dots of coloured light called pixels. This archaeopteryx shows how pixels make up a picture.

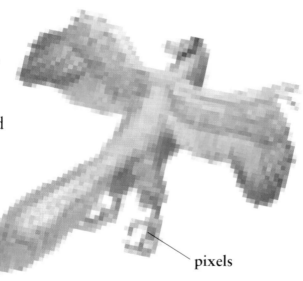

pixels

◁ You move a mouse around to point at things on the screen. A cursor on the screen follows your movements.

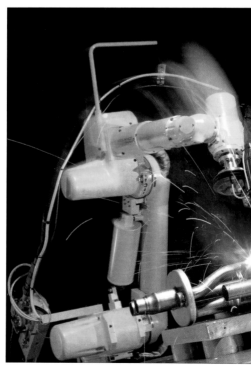

△ This is a robot that puts car parts together in a factory. It is controlled by a computer that has been programmed to tell the robot what to do.

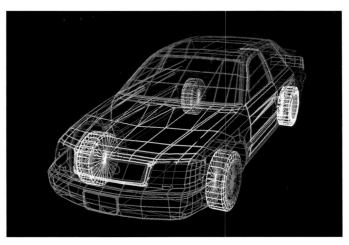

△ Engineers use computers to design cars. The picture on the screen shows what the car will look like when it is built.

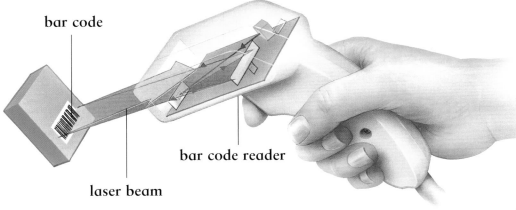

bar code

bar code reader

laser beam

◁ Bar codes are patterns of black and white stripes. They contain coded information about the objects they are printed on, such as the price. A laser beam scans the bar code and sends the information to a computer. You can see an example of this in a supermarket.

◁ With a headset like this you can have the feeling of being in another world – perhaps among the dinosaurs, or in Ancient Rome. This is called virtual reality. The headset shows pictures of the world created by the computer. It also plays sounds made by the people and animals in that world.

Find out more
Calculator
Electricity
Mathematics
Numbers
Technology

Conservation

Many animals are in danger of dying out, or becoming extinct. This may be because their habitat has been destroyed or polluted, or because they have been hunted. It is important that we conserve these animals and their homes.

△ Rubbish pollutes the environment. It is also dangerous to animals, who may get trapped inside empty cans and bottles. Collecting rubbish is an excellent way of helping animals.

△ Corncrakes nest in fields and many used to die when farmers cut their crops. New ways of harvesting are now helping them to survive.

△ Dodos once lived on the island of Mauritius, but because they could not fly they were easily hunted by sailors visiting the island. In 1680, the dodo became extinct.

▽ In the last 50 years the survival of whales has been threatened by over-hunting. Nowadays, whale hunting is carefully controlled.

Find out more
Panda
Tiger

Coral reef

Coral reefs are found in shallow tropical seas. They look like underwater gardens, but the corals are not flowers – they are huge groups of tiny animals called polyps and their skeletons.

△ Coral reefs can stretch for thousands of kilometres. The biggest of all is the Great Barrier Reef off the coast of northeast Australia.

▽ A coral reef is home to an amazing variety of animals, from the conger eel and giant clam (bottom left) to the striped angelfish and coral-eating parrotfish above them. The reef gives them shelter from predators and is the source of food.

◁ A coral polyp has tentacles covered with stinging cells, which it uses to stun any tiny creature that passes by. As it grows, the polyp builds a cup-like skeleton around itself. When it dies, this is the only thing that remains. The reef is made up of millions of these tiny skeletons.

Find out more

Eel
Seahorse
Shellfish
Starfish

Cow and Bull

Female cattle are called cows and the males are called bulls. They are kept on farms all over the world for their meat, called beef, and for their milk. We also use their hides (skin) to make leather shoes and clothes.

Friesian cow

Jersey cow

Hereford bull

Highland cow

△ Female cattle that are reared for their milk are called dairy cows. Twice a day they are brought in from the fields to be milked. Special machines suck the milk from the cow's udder.

△ Although they are not clever animals, cattle are very strong. In many parts of the world, they are used to pull ploughs and carts.

△ There are over 250 breeds of cattle, and each has its own qualities. Friesians give a lot of milk. Jerseys are famous for their rich, creamy milk. Herefords are often used as beef cattle. Highland cattle are tough enough to survive cold winters.

Find out more
Pig

Crab

Crabs are creatures with ten legs and a hard shell. Most live in the sea or along the shore, where they scurry sideways. Their two front legs are frightening pincers, used for feeding and fighting off attackers.

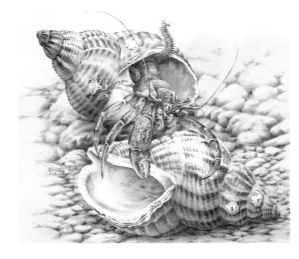

△ Hermit crabs do not have their own shells, but live in the empty shells of sea snails and whelks. As a hermit crab grows, it moves into bigger shells.

▽ Tropical horseshoe crabs are a very ancient species, related to spiders and scorpions. They emerge from the sea in large numbers to lay eggs on the shore.

◁ The legs of some crabs are adapted for swimming. The back legs of this swimmer crab are flattened like tiny paddles.

▷ Fiddler crabs live in muddy mangrove swamps in all regions of the world. One of the male fiddler crab's claws is huge. He waves it to attract females to his burrow.

Find out more
Scorpion
Spider

Cricket and Grasshopper

Crickets and grasshoppers are insects that prefer to hop on their long back legs rather than fly. Males 'sing' to attract mates – grasshoppers do this by rubbing their back legs together, while crickets use their wings.

△ Many grasshoppers are brightly coloured. This warns predators that the grasshopper can spit a nasty-tasting protective foam.

◁ Grasshoppers have very strong muscles in their long back legs and a remarkable spring in their knees. The grasshopper can jump 12 times its own length – this would be like a child jumping over a house!

△ Locusts are a kind of grasshopper found in Africa. Every now and then they form huge swarms, which destroy crops.

▽ Bush crickets, like this great green bush cricket, are known as katydids because the male's song sounds like someone saying, 'Katy did'. Females have slit-like ears in their front legs, which they use to listen to the singing males.

Fact box

• Crickets and grasshoppers eat leaves and grasses. Some eat other insects too.
• Each species has its own special song.
• People used to keep crickets in cages to hear them sing.

Find out more
Beetle
Dragonfly
and Damselfly
Insect

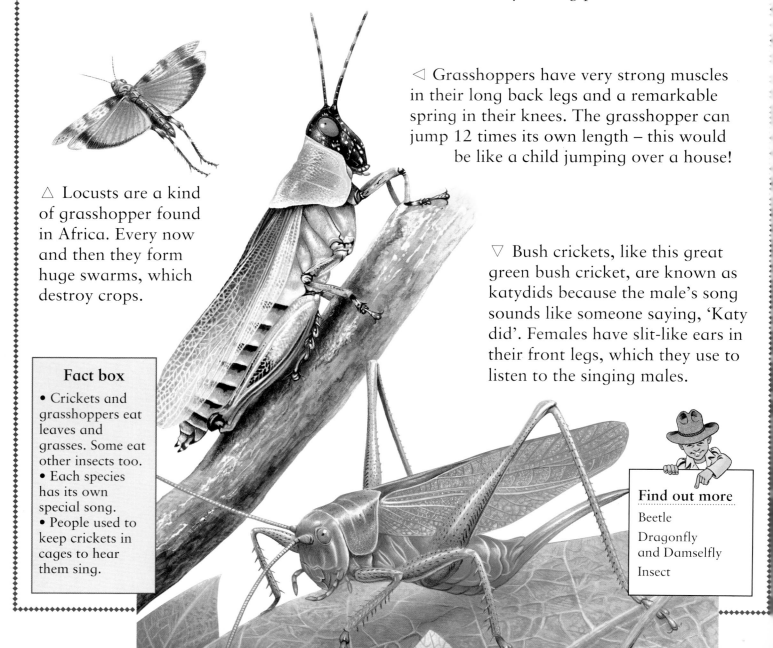

Dance

ballet shoes

When you dance, you move your body in time to music. You may follow a pattern of steps, or just twist and twirl and stamp your feet to fit the music. People all over the world love to dance. Many dancers tell a story with their hands and bodies instead of words.

◁ This Indian dancer moves her hands and fingers in a special way to tell a story about Hindu gods.

▷ Most ballet dancers first learn to dance when they are very young. They learn special positions for their hands and feet.

◁ Spanish flamenco dancers stamp and tap their heels and toes. They move their hands, while twisting and turning their bodies in time to guitar music.

▷ These Russian folk dancers leap up high and kick out their legs to fast music.

Find out more
Art and artists
Asia
Europe
Music
Religion

79

Day and Night

Days and nights happen because the Earth spins as it travels around the Sun. The Sun shines onto the side of the Earth facing it. As the Earth spins, different parts of the Earth's surface get more or less sunlight. When the part of the Earth you live on is in the sunlight, you have day.

◁ Most people sleep at night and play or work in the day. But some animals, such as owls, sleep by day and look for food at night. They are called nocturnal.

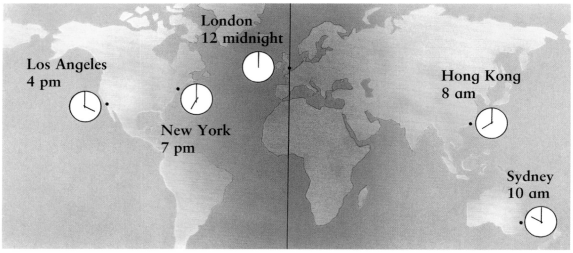

Los Angeles
4 pm

London
12 midnight

New York
7 pm

Hong Kong
8 am

Sydney
10 am

△ When it is day where you are, it is night on the other side of the world. The time changes as you travel around the world.

◁ Try this experiment to see how day and night happen. Work with a friend in a dark room. Shine a torch on one side of a globe. The other person turns the globe slowly around. Can you see how each part of the globe is in the light for a time, while the rest is in shadow?

Find out more
Clocks
Earth
Living things
Seasons
Solar System

Deep-sea fish

Down at the bottom of the sea the water is cold and dark. Food is scarce and fish here must prey on one another or eat dead fish. Deep-sea fish are quite small, but they often have huge, gaping jaws and stretchy stomachs to make the most of any food going.

▷ The gulper can completely unhinge its huge jaws so it can swallow larger fish. It also has a stomach that expands to cope with the largest of meals.

▽ Tube worms called riftia live in the hot waters gushing from volcanic vents on the seabed. They eat bacteria that feed on sulphur from the hot vents.

▽ Like many fish in the dark depths, the anglerfish makes its own light. The female anglerfish's light dangles on a long stalk-like fin in front of her mouth, to lure prey into her jaws. The male has no 'fishing fin' and relies on the female to eat. He bites into her and feeds on her blood.

anglerfish

gulper eel

riftia

dragonfish

◁ Dragonfish have eyes, but they find their food in the dark by waving their long feelers through the water.

Find out more
Eel
Fish
Shark

Deer

Deer come in all shapes and sizes, from the tiny puda to the large moose. They are graceful mammals that can run swiftly from danger. Deer are found in the Northern Hemisphere and South America.

△ **1** Make a cast of a deer hoof-print to keep forever. First take a piece of card six centimetres wide and 50 centimetres long. Bend the card into a circle around the hoofprint and fasten with tape.

△ **2** Mix some plaster of Paris powder with water to make a thick paste. Pour the paste into the card mould until it reaches just below the top of the card.

△ Each year, male deer grow a new set of antlers. During the breeding season, they fight fierce battles with each other to become leader of the herd.

△ **3** Leave it until it sets hard, then carefully lift off the plaster in its mould. Take home your cast and remove the card. Using an old toothbrush, clean off any soil from the plaster cast.

Find out more
Antelope
Elk
Mammal
Reindeer

Desert

A desert is a dry place where little or no rain falls. Few people live there. Only tough plants and animals can live in these rocky or sandy places. Some deserts are blazing hot during the day and freezing cold at night. Other deserts are cold most of the time.

△ Monument Valley is in North America. Sand is blown about by strong winds and this has worn the rocks into these strange shapes.

▷ These people are nomads. This means that they move around to find food and water. They often live in tents that can be moved easily.

desert scorpion

△ The scorpion is a deadly hunter. It has a poisonous sting in its tail.

prickly pear cactus

camel

◁ A camel can travel a long way without food and water. It lives on fat which is stored in its hump.

◁ Cactus plants store water in their thick stems. The spines protect them

Find out more

Africa
Antarctica and Arctic
Asia
North America
Plants

Dinosaurs

Dinosaurs lived on Earth millions of years ago. These scaly-skinned reptiles were all shapes and sizes. There were huge creatures that weighed ten times as much as an elephant, and others the size of chickens. Some were fierce meat-eaters and some only ate plants.

△ Scientists study fossils of dinosaur footprints. They can use them to work out how they moved and how fast they ran.

◁ Dinosaurs laid eggs just like reptiles do today. Maiasaura laid eggs in a nest. This dinosaur cared for her babies after they hatched.

Fact box

• The word dinosaur means terrible lizard.

• Dinosaurs lived on Earth long before the first human beings.

• Dinosaurs became extinct about 65 million years ago. We do not know why they died out.

Maiasaura
(**My**-a-**saw**-ra)

▷ You can visit a museum to find out about dinosaurs. This is the skeleton of Tyrannosaurus rex. Scientists have studied its bones and teeth to find out how it lived.

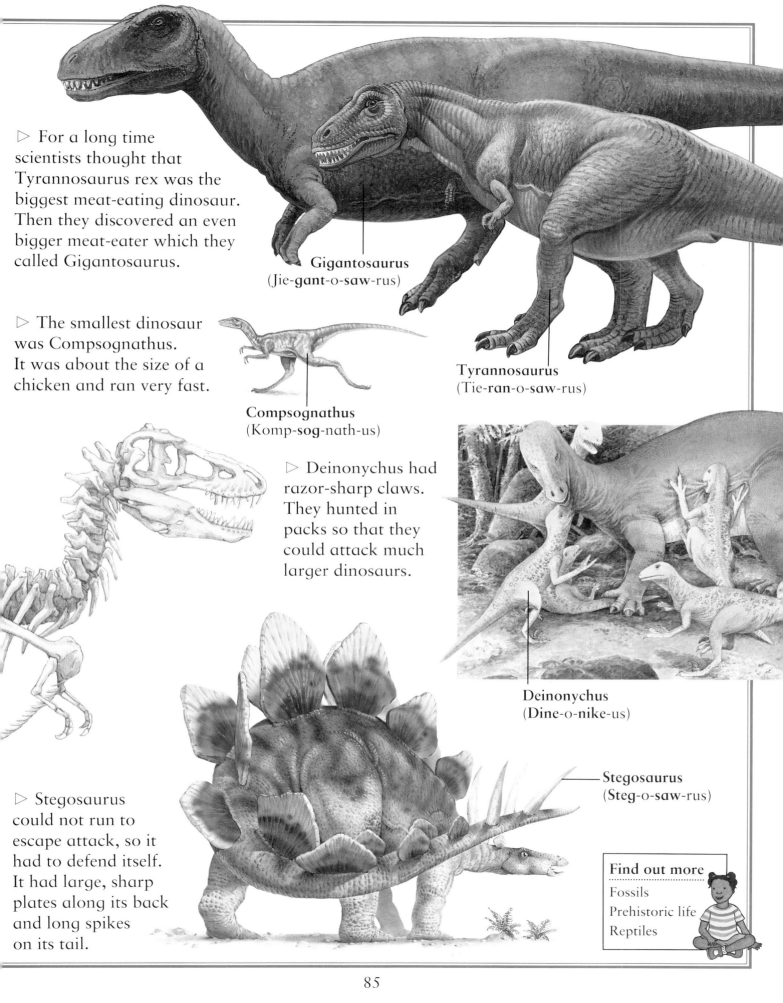

▷ For a long time scientists thought that Tyrannosaurus rex was the biggest meat-eating dinosaur. Then they discovered an even bigger meat-eater which they called Gigantosaurus.

Gigantosaurus
(Jie-**gant**-o-**saw**-rus)

Tyrannosaurus
(Tie-**ran**-o-**saw**-rus)

▷ The smallest dinosaur was Compsognathus. It was about the size of a chicken and ran very fast.

Compsognathus
(Komp-**sog**-nath-us)

▷ Deinonychus had razor-sharp claws. They hunted in packs so that they could attack much larger dinosaurs.

Deinonychus
(Dine-o-**nike**-us)

Stegosaurus
(Steg-o-**saw**-rus)

▷ Stegosaurus could not run to escape attack, so it had to defend itself. It had large, sharp plates along its back and long spikes on its tail.

Find out more
Fossils
Prehistoric life
Reptiles

Dog (domestic)

Dogs were domesticated about 12,000 years ago, when cavemen first tamed the Asiatic wolf. Since then, dogs have lived with people wherever they have travelled. Over time they have been bred to help people both in their everyday lives and in their work.

Bernese mountain dog

Labrador

Yorkshire terrier

▷ There are about 400 dog breeds, which are divided into seven groups. These are: sporting dogs; hounds; working dogs; terriers; toy dogs; non-sporting dogs; and herding dogs. The Bernese mountain dog is a working dog, the Labrador is a sporting dog and the Yorkshire terrier is a toy dog.

▽▷ The collie (below) and the corgi (right) are both herding dogs. Collies help to round up sheep. Corgis once helped to herd cattle. Many collies work on farms, but most corgis are now just pets.

△ Dogs kept as pets should be taught to walk on a lead and house-trained. They must be looked after properly throughout their lives.

Find out more
Cat (domestic)
Dog (wild)
Fox
Hyena

Dog (wild)

In many ways wild dogs look and behave like domestic dogs, and they are related. However, wild dogs are usually afraid of humans and cannot be trained. These meat-eaters often live in packs and are found all over the world.

▷ Like most wild dogs, the Cape hunting dogs of East Africa are fierce killers. They have long front teeth for piercing or tearing, and sharp cheek teeth for slicing meat into small chunks. They work in teams to chase down antelope, zebra and wildebeest.

◁ Wild dogs rely on their sense of smell and sharp hearing for hunting. Once they have found their prey's scent, they give chase. Like other dogs, North American coyotes (left) howl to call up the pack for a hunt.

Fact box

• The dhole of India can kill bears and even tigers.
• Golden jackals of southeastern Europe now live mostly on human rubbish.
• The coyote is sometimes called the prairie wolf.

◁ Jackals live in Africa and Asia. They hunt mainly alone at night, and form packs only when there is a chance of sharing a lion's kill.

Find out more
Dog (domestic)
Fox

Dolphin

Dolphins are intelligent, graceful sea creatures. They are not fish, but mammals and, like us, they breathe air. They make clicking sounds to help them find their way, catch their prey and communicate.

white-sided dolphin

△ There are over 30 species of dolphin, found in seas all over the world.

Fact box
• A dolphin's top speed is 40 kilometres per hour.
• A dolphin breathes through a blowhole in the top of its head.

spotted dolphin

◁ Dolphins send out sounds in pulses. Then they listen for echoes reflected back from nearby objects to find out what is around them. This way, they can track down fish to eat.

▽ Bottle-nosed dolphins love to play. Like many other dolphin species, their streamlined shape and powerful tails help them speed through the water and they often jump high into the air. They live in big family groups called schools, and like to race alongside boats.

bottle-nosed dolphin

Find out more
Killer whale

Donkey

Patient and strong, donkeys are used all over the world to carry people and goods. Their small feet and thick coats make them suited to working in dry, rocky places. Because they are quiet animals and are gentle with children, donkeys are often kept as pets.

Fact box
• Donkeys live for up to 40 years.
• Donkeys can be used for pulling carts as well as for riding.
• A female donkey is called a jenny, a male is called a jack.
• Mules are a cross between a male donkey and a female horse.

▽ Donkeys range in colour from almost white to nearly black. They usually have two dark stripes running along their backs and across their shoulders. Unlike horses, only the ends of their tails have long hairs.

▽ Donkeys are descended from wild asses that were tamed by the ancient Egyptians. Wild asses look very similar to donkeys, with large pointed ears and small hooves. They have thin black stripes on their legs, unlike donkeys.

▽ Donkeys are usually good workers. They can also be stubborn and will make a loud braying noise if they are angry or upset.

Find out more
Horse
Zebra

Dragonfly and Damselfly

Dragonflies are the fastest flying insects, swooping over the streams and ponds where they live at up to 90 kilometres per hour. Damselflies are thinner and more delicate, with a slow, fluttering flight.

△ Dragonflies and damselflies live near water. The young, called nymphs, hatch from eggs laid on plants. They feed on other water creatures, and after two years the nymphs grow into adults.

▷ The wings of the damselfly are almost transparent. They shimmer as the damselfly searches for small insects to eat.

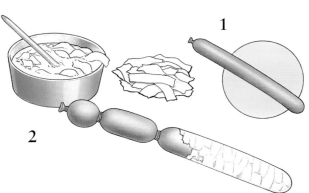

△ **1** To make a model dragonfly start by blowing up a long balloon. **2** Twist and tie the balloon twice to make the three body sections, then cover the balloon with several layers of papier mâché. When this is dry, paint the body.

▷ **3** Make the wings from wire bent into shape. Cover them with clear cling film, then fasten them to the body with some more wire. Attach pipe cleaners or straws to the middle section for the legs. For the eyes, cut a ping-pong ball in half and glue it to the head.

Find out more
Ant and Termite
Bee and Wasp
Beetle
Fly
Insect

Drama

Drama is a story told in words and actions. Most dramas are called plays. They are performed by actors on a stage in front of an audience. Most plays are performed in a theatre. You can also watch drama on the television and in the cinema, or listen to it on the radio.

◁ Puppets can be used instead of people to perform plays. These puppets are from India.

▷ You could put on your own play. Decide on a story and make some scenery. Dress up in costumes and put on make-up. Then ask people to come along and watch.

△ This woman is a mime artist. She uses her body to tell a story without words.

◁ Kabuki is a type of play performed in Japan. All the actors are men. They wear colourful costumes and lots of make-up.

Find out more

History
Jobs
Stories

Duck and Goose

Ducks and geese are water birds. Members of this family live in most parts of the world. They have thick plumage (feathers) to keep them warm, and webbed feet for paddling along in water.

△ Geese are generally bigger than ducks and have longer necks. Geese have big beaks for pulling up and eating grass. Ducks have flatter beaks for sifting food from the water.

△ Eider ducks breed along icy northern coasts. To keep her eggs warm the female lines the nest with fluffy feathers (down) plucked from her breast.

◁ Ducks have short legs and they waddle when they walk. Their feet have three front toes in a web and a rear toe that is free. Almost all duck species live in fresh water. As well as feeding on insects and worms, they eat vegetable matter.

▽ Most Canada geese that breed in Canada and Alaska migrate to Mexico and the southern United States in winter. When they fly, they often make a honking noise.

△ Male ducks are called drakes. They often have colourful plumage, which is designed to attract females. Female ducks are usually dull brown.

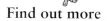

Find out more
Bird
Gull
Migration
Pelican
Swan

Eagle

Strong wings, sharp eyes and powerful talons make eagles great hunters. Their large, hooked bills are used for slicing open and eating – not for killing. They also scavenge if they find dead animals. These big birds of prey are found in regions from the Arctic to the tropics.

◁ The golden eagle (left) and the white-tailed sea eagle are the most widespread eagle species. They are found in Europe and northern Asia. Like most eagles, they nest on cliffs, raising one or two chicks a year.

△ The North American bald eagle is the national bird of the United States. It is not really bald, but has contrasting white head and brown body feathers. It lives close to lakes, rivers and coasts.

Fact box
• Because they are so strong, eagles have been symbols of war and national power for thousands of years.
• Eagles mate for life and return to use the same nest every year.

▷ Harpy eagles come from the jungles of South America and the South Pacific. They are powerful hunters, eating sloths, macaws and monkeys. The great harpy eagle (right) is the largest eagle.

Find out more
Bird
Owl
Sea bird
Vulture

Earth

The Earth is the planet we live on. It formed about 4.5 billion years ago from a cloud of dust, rock and gas. Over millions of years since then, volcanoes, earthquakes, wind and rain have changed its surface. Scientists think the Earth is the only planet in the Solar System where plants and animals can live.

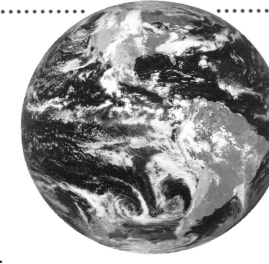

△ Two-thirds of the Earth is covered in salty sea water. Around the Earth is a blanket of air, called the atmosphere.

▽ The Earth is a giant ball of rock. Beneath the surface, this rock is so hot that some of it is molten (melted) and runny. Around the outside, the rock forms a hard crust.

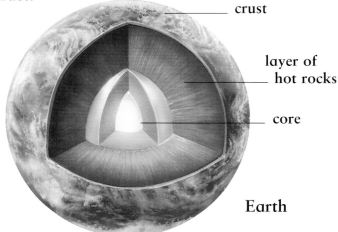

crust

layer of hot rocks

core

Earth

▷ Millions of years ago, the land on Earth was joined together in one huge continent. Gradually, it split up and formed the continents we have today. These are still moving slowly. Millions of years from now, the surface of the Earth will look very different from the way it does today.

▽ The Earth's crust is made up of enormous sections called plates. These move very, very slowly. Sometimes they push against each other and crumple. When this happens, mountains form.

Fact box
• People once thought that the Earth was flat and you could fall off the edge.

Find out more
Air and
Atmosphere
Day and Night
Solar System
Volcano
Water
Weather

Eel

Because they are long and thin, and have wriggly bodies, you may think that eels are a type of snake. In fact, they are fish. Like fish, they are scaly and have thin fins that run the length of their bodies.

▷ The moray eel can grow up to three metres long. It hides by day in holes in the rocks, and only comes out at night. It eats shellfish but will attack humans if disturbed.

▽ To breed, freshwater eels have to swim thousands of kilometres – from lakes and rivers in America and Europe, to the Sargasso Sea, near Bermuda. The eels' eggs hatch there and drift north in an ocean current. Up to three years later the young eels wriggle back into the rivers again.

Fact box

• Young eels are called elvers.
• There are about 600 kinds of eel, living in fresh- and saltwater all over the world.
• To reach lakes further inland, freshwater eels slither overland across damp grass.

△ The electric eel of South America eats small fish. It catches them by stunning the fish with an electric shock. This shock is so strong that it could knock down a human.

Find out more
Goldfish and Carp
Shellfish

Electrical current

Electrical energy moves along wires. When it flows along a wire this is called an electric current. Electricity is used to make heat, light, sound and movement – it can make all kinds of machines work. Electricity can be stored in batteries too.

△ You can make static electricity. Rub a balloon on a jumper. The static will make it stick to the wall.

 Never play with, or go near, electrical sockets. Electricity can kill you.

▷ To light the bulb, electricity flows from the battery down the wire through the bulb and back to the battery. This is called a circuit.

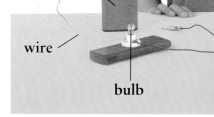

battery

wire

bulb

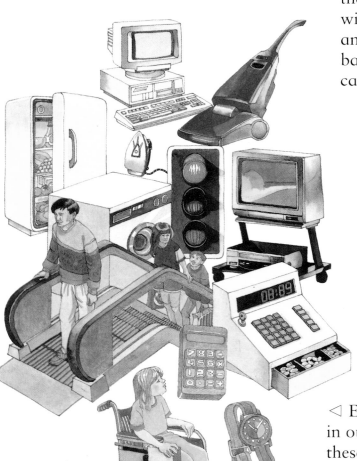

◁ Electricity is important in our daily lives. None of these machines could work without it. They all use electricity.

Find out more
Cars
Energy
Light
Trains
Weather

96

Electricity

Electricity is a form of energy. It is also known as electrical energy. We get some electricity from batteries, but most of the electricity in our homes is made in generating stations. It reaches our homes along thick cables. The electricity flows along these, like a current in a stream. This is why we call it current electricity. Electricity that does not flow in a current is called static electricity.

△ A flash of lightning is a huge spark of electricity. Static electricity forms in clouds and jumps through the air. It may travel from cloud to cloud, or down to the ground.

▽ Run a plastic comb through your hair quickly, several times. Hold the comb over some bits of paper and see how it attracts the paper. Combing your hair made static electricity form on the comb. Static electricity on an object can make it attract other objects.

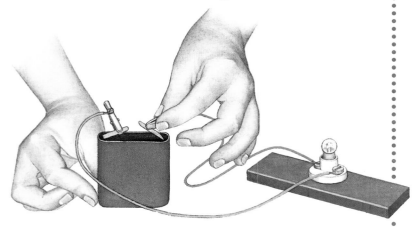

△ Electricity only flows along wires if they are joined in a loop called a circuit. In a torch, a circuit joins one end of a battery to the other, through a bulb and a switch. The circuit here works in the same way. The bulb will only light up if there is no gap anywhere in the circuit.

▷ Tall towers called pylons hold up thick electrical wires, or cables. These carry electricity from generating stations to towns and cities. When it gets there, it travels along cables buried under the ground.

Fact box

• Tall buildings and church spires often have a metal rod leading from the top to the ground. This is called a lightning conductor. If the building is struck by lightning, the conductor carries the electricity safely to the ground.

◁ These model cars are controlled by changing the amount of electricity flowing in the metal race track. In many machines, the flow of electricity is controlled using electronics, which are very tiny but complicated circuits.

▽ There is an electric motor in this model train. Electricity flows along the metal tracks and into the train. It makes the motor spin, and this moves the wheels of the train. When the electricity stops, the train stops.

Find out more
Battery
Calculator
Computers
Energy
Magnets

Elephant

Elephants are the heaviest land animals. They are also intelligent and have good memories. There are two species: one lives in Africa, another in India. They use their long trunks almost like an arm, to put food and water in their mouths. Their tusks are made of ivory and males use them for fighting.

△ In India, elephants are trained to do heavy work, such as lifting logs. An elephant driver or keeper is called a mahout.

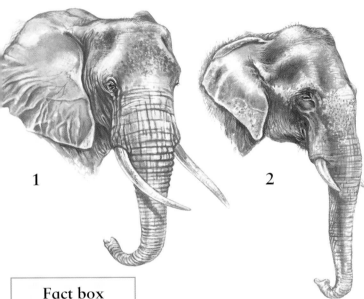

1

2

◁ 1 The African elephant is bigger than its Indian cousin. It has bigger tusks and ears and a hollow forehead. The tusks are really teeth that grow outside the mouth.
◁ 2 The Indian elephant has smaller ears and a rounded forehead. Only the male Indian elephant has tusks.

▽ In Africa, elephants live in small family groups ruled by the oldest females. Males live in all-male herds.

Fact box
• African elephants grow to four metres, over twice as tall as an adult human.
• They weigh as much as seven tonnes – heavier than six cars.
• Elephants can live to be 70.

Find out more
Giraffe
Hippopotamus
Rhinoceros

Elk

There are two kinds of elk. One lives in Canada and the United States; the other lives in northern Europe and looks like the American moose. They are both large members of the deer family.

△ The American elk is known as a wapiti. Wapiti are closely related to the red deer of Europe. Like all deer, wapiti mainly eat fresh shoots and fruit.

▷ European elks are usually born as twins in the spring. They are unsteady on their feet at first but are soon able to trot at a fast pace.

▷ American elk calves are born in the spring. Their white-spotted coats act as camouflage and help them hide from wolves and pumas.

◁ Male elks (bulls) grow huge spoon-shaped antlers. They use them to challenge other males and show off to the females. The older the male, the larger his antlers. The mating season in autumn is called the rut. At this time, male elks fill the air with low grunting noises.

Find out more
Deer
Mammal
Reindeer

Energy

Nothing can happen without energy. Energy is what makes everything work, including you. There are many different types of energy. There is movement energy, light energy, heat energy, chemical energy and electrical energy. Energy can change from one type to another. But it cannot be made from scratch or destroyed.

△ Sound is a type of energy. Beating the drum makes a sound which travels through the air in waves. When the waves reach your ears, you hear the sound.

△ This is New York. In a big city like this, huge amounts of energy are needed to heat, light, and give power to offices and homes, and to make buses, cars and trains run.

▽ Plants use energy from sunshine to make food for themselves. All living things, including plants and animals, need energy from food to stay alive. Some animals eat plants, some eat other animals and some eat both. In the end, all plants and animals get the energy they need from the Sun.

energy from the Sun

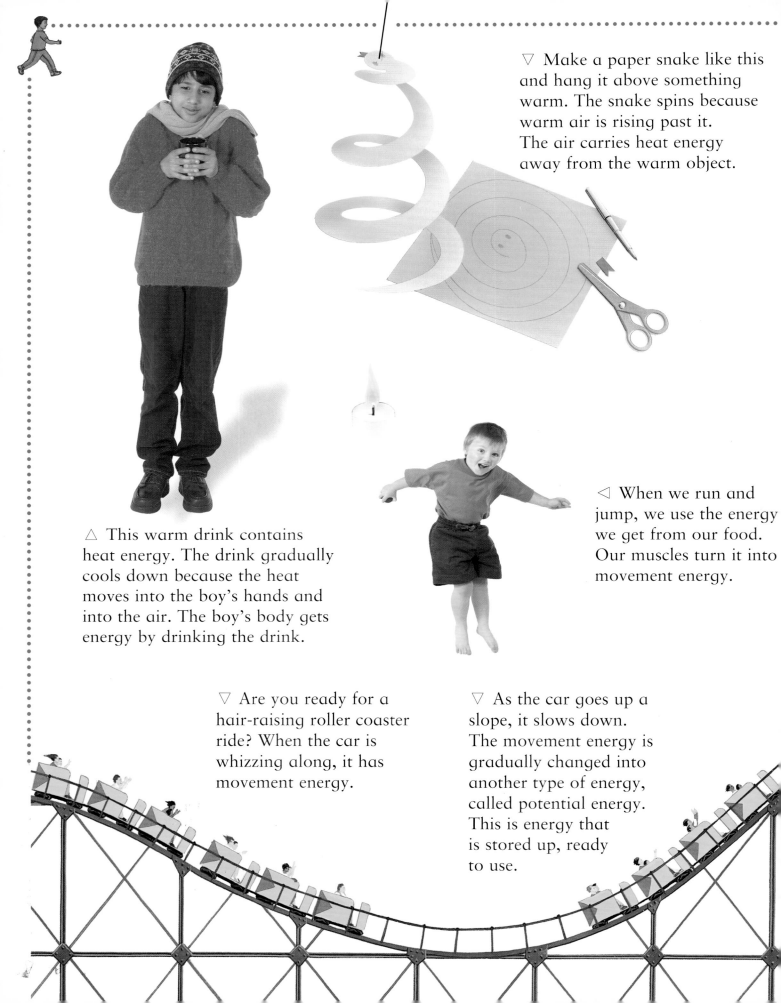

▽ Make a paper snake like this and hang it above something warm. The snake spins because warm air is rising past it. The air carries heat energy away from the warm object.

△ This warm drink contains heat energy. The drink gradually cools down because the heat moves into the boy's hands and into the air. The boy's body gets energy by drinking the drink.

◁ When we run and jump, we use the energy we get from our food. Our muscles turn it into movement energy.

▽ Are you ready for a hair-raising roller coaster ride? When the car is whizzing along, it has movement energy.

▽ As the car goes up a slope, it slows down. The movement energy is gradually changed into another type of energy, called potential energy. This is energy that is stored up, ready to use.

▽ Wind is air with movement energy. The blades of these wind turbines catch the movement energy from the air, and the turbines turn it into electrical energy.

△ Deep under the Earth's crust, the rock is very hot. In some places, there is hot rock near the surface, too. The heat energy in the rock can be very useful. Water is pumped through the rock, so it gets hot. Then it is piped into homes. This kind of energy is called geothermal energy.

▷ For thousands of years, people have used the heat energy and light energy from fire. We still use it to cook food and keep us warm.

△ As you hurtle down the slope again, you soon gather speed. The potential energy is changing back into movement energy.

Fact box

• You could run 2 kilometres on the energy you get from eating a chocolate bar – but only 50 metres on the energy you get from eating a lettuce leaf.

ancient forest

◁ We get a lot of energy from burning coal, oil and gas. These lie under the ground or under the sea bed. They formed millions of years ago from the remains of plants and animals. Ancient remains of plants and animals are called fossils, so the fuels are called fossil fuels.

coal – the remains of an ancient forest

1

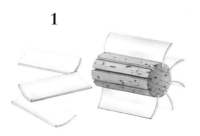

2

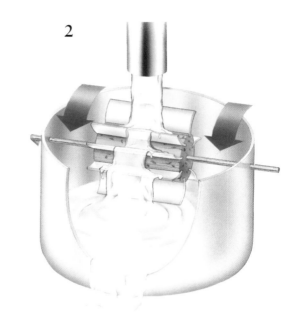

△ **1** You can use the energy in falling water to turn a water wheel. Ask an adult to cut slots in a cork and rectangles from a plastic bottle. Slide the rectangles into the slots to make paddles.

▷ There is a special kind of water wheel, called a turbine, inside this dam. Water flows from behind the dam and makes the turbine turn. This turns a machine called a generator, which changes the movement energy into electrical energy.

◁ **2** Push two pieces of stiff wire into the cork, one at each end, as the picture shows. (Ask an adult to help you.) Hold the wheel under a tap and run the water over it. The wheel spins. This movement energy can be used to power machines or make electricity.

Find out more

Electricity
Engines
Force
Fuels
Machines
Melting and
Boiling
Nuclear energy

Engines

Many machines have engines to make them work. For example, a car has an engine which makes its wheels turn. A ship has an engine that turns propellers in the water. A jet aircraft's engines push it through the air. All these engines needs fuel to work. The engine turns the energy in the fuel into movement energy.

Fact box
• The power of an engine is measured in units called horsepower. This word was invented by the first engineers, who compared engine power to horse power.

Petrol engine

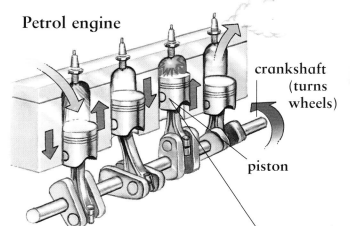

crankshaft (turns wheels)

piston

△ A rocket engine makes a stream of hot gas. The stream rushes out of the base of the rocket. It pushes the rocket upwards.

Close-up of a piston

spark plug (makes the spark)

explosion

piston

△ Inside a car engine are pistons that move up and down in cylinders. A mixture of petrol and air is sucked into the cylinder. The mixture explodes when the spark plug makes a spark, pushing the piston down. The cylinders move down one after the other, turning the crankshaft.

Steam locomotive

◁ This old locomotive had a steam engine. Fire in the engine boiled water to make steam. This pushed pistons in and out, turning the wheels.

Find out more
Energy
Flight
Fuels
Machines
Water

Europe

Europe is the second smallest continent – only Australia is smaller. It stretches from the snowy Arctic in the north to the warm lands of the Mediterranean Sea in the south. It has high mountains, large forests and many rivers. Many people live in Europe and some parts are very crowded. Most people live in or near cities.

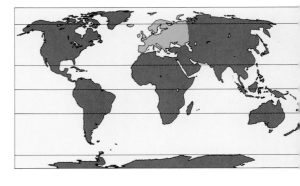

△ Europe is shown in green on this map. Europe has a ragged outline. In the east it is joined to Asia.

◁ The peacock butterfly is found in gardens, woods and mountains all over Europe, except in the cold north.

peacock butterfly

▽ St Basil's Cathedral is in Moscow, the capital city of Russia. Russia is the largest country in the world. It stretches across Europe and Asia.

△ A beach in Amalfi, Italy in southern Europe. Millions of tourists come to enjoy a holiday in the warm waters around the Mediterranean Sea.

▽ Along the coast of Norway, in northern Europe, there are deep inlets of sea with steep sides, called fjords.

◁ In Sweden, people dance around a maypole on Midsummer's Eve to mark the return of summer.

▷ Olive trees grow in rows on the hot, dry hills of southern Spain. Lots of Mediterranean countries grow olives and many other fruits.

◁ The Danube River flows through the middle of Budapest, the capital of Hungary. Like many European cities, Budapest has lots of fine old buildings in its centre.

Find out more
History
World

Evolution

Millions of years have passed since life first started on Earth. The animals that lived then are very different from those that are found now. This is because things evolve (change) over time to stand a better chance of survival.

△ **1** Fossils are the remains of animals that died millions of years ago. They are a good way of telling how things have evolved. You can find fossils on some beaches and in certain types of rock formations.

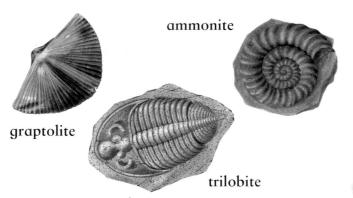

ammonite

graptolite

trilobite

△ **2** Look at fossils with a magnifying glass. You will see that they look quite similar to some animals still alive today. The way they have changed shows how they have evolved in order to survive.

◁ Once there was just one type of fox, but new forms evolved. The Arctic fox has thick fur to keep warm, and is coloured white for camouflage.

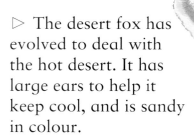

▷ The desert fox has evolved to deal with the hot desert. It has large ears to help it keep cool, and is sandy in colour.

◁ The peppered moth has evolved very recently. Usually this moth is light coloured but a black-winged form is found in places where the trees have been blackened by smoke from factories. This gives it better camouflage.

Find out more
Bird
Camouflage
Habitat

Experiment

Scientists are always trying to find out more about the world we live in. They try out their ideas using tests, called experiments. Some experiments are very quick and easy to do. Others are very long and complicated. Some do not work well the first time and have to be done again. Here is an experiment you can do. It is a test to see which ball bounces best.

△ **1** You will need different kinds of balls. For example, you could use a tennis ball and a soft sponge ball. You will also need to make a measure and mark it in metres or feet.

▷ **4** Study your results. What do they show? Before you did the experiment, did you guess how high each ball would bounce? Were you right?

◁ **2** Get a friend to hold the measure upright. Now drop each ball from the same height. Before you drop a ball, try guessing how high it will bounce.

Find out more

Biology
Chemistry and Chemicals
Energy
Physics

△ **3** Note the type of ball and how high it bounces. Write down your results. Do this for each ball in turn.

Farming

All over the world, farmers grow crops and raise animals for food. They plant fields of wheat, rice, corn, oats and vegetables. They raise animals for their meat, milk and eggs. Large farms use machines to do much of the work. Other farms do all the work by hand.

bread

pasta

▽ Rice is an important crop in China, India and other countries in Asia. It is grown in flooded fields called paddies. It is usually sown and picked by hand.

▷ Wheat is usually grown in huge fields. It is harvested by a combine harvester. Wheat grain is ground up into flour to make bread and pasta.

rice

△ Milk from cows is used to make dairy produce such as cheese, butter and cream.

△ Female chickens are called hens. They lay eggs. People eat chickens' eggs and meat.

Fact box

• Farming began 10,000 years ago. Before then people survived by hunting animals and gathering plants.

• Two of the most widely eaten foods are rice and potatoes.

• Over half of the world's people eat rice at every meal.

◁ Large flocks of sheep are raised on sheep stations in New Zealand and Australia. Their wool is clipped off, cleaned and spun into yarn.

◁ Pests, such as the Colorado beetle, destroy crops. Farmers spray the crops with chemicals to kill the pests.

△ This tractor is spreading manure over a ploughed field. Manure is a fertilizer. It feeds the soil and helps new crops to grow large and strong.

Find out more

Asia

Australia and the Pacific Islands

Conservation

Europe

— Colorado beetle

Fish

Fish live in water and are all different shapes and sizes. The enormous whale shark can be up to 15 metres long. A tiny fish called a pygmy goby is no longer than your fingernail. Some fish live in warm, shallow water. Others live in the cold, deep sea.

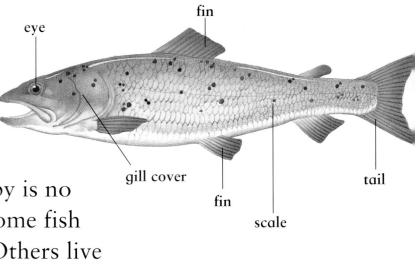

eye

fin

gill cover

fin

scale

tail

great white shark

◁ Great white sharks are fast swimmers and fierce hunters. They use their razor-sharp teeth to tear apart their prey.

▽ Blue marlin and many other big fish live far away from the shore. Tuna and mackerel live close to the surface. Sawfish and rays live on the sea bed.

blue marlin

tuna

mackerel

ray

sawfish

puffer fish

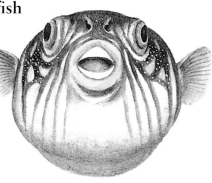

▷ A puffer fish can blow up its body like a balloon. It does this to scare away its enemies.

African cichlid

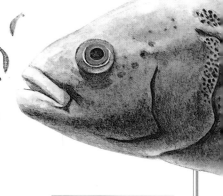

▷ The babies of the African cichlid fish swim into their mother's mouth to escape from danger.

Fact box

• A fish is a vertebrate, which means that it has a backbone.
• They breathe by taking in oxygen from the water through their gills.
• Most fish swim through the water by moving their tails from side to side.

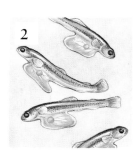
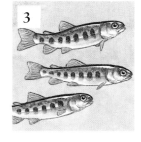

△ 1 A female salmon lays her eggs in a river. 2 When the eggs hatch, the babies are called fry.

△ 3 The young salmon live in the river for over two years. 4 Then they swim down to the sea.

▽ Fish that live in the warm, shallow water around coral reefs are often brightly coloured. Their bold patterns help them to hide among the corals and to creep up on their prey.

lion fish

angel fish

parrot fish

butterfly fish

cowfish

Find out more

Animals
Food
Oceans and seas
Prehistoric life
Water

Flamingo, Heron and Stork

Flamingos live in colonies on shallow lakes in Africa, South America and Asia. They are pink with large wings, slim necks and long, thin legs for wading in water. The largest is the great flamingo, which is 1.5 metres tall. Flamingos, herons and storks are all in the same group of birds.

▽ Herons are long legged like flamingos. They wade along the edges of lakes and rivers, hunting for fish. When they spot one, they spear it with their sharp beak. Like most wading birds, they often stand on one leg. This keeps the leg out of the water warm.

△ Flamingos wade through the shallows moving their heads from side to side. Their specially shaped beaks act like sieves, filtering shrimps and other tiny animals from the muddy water. Flamingos get their pink colour from the shrimps they eat.

▽ Storks are also wading birds. White storks spend the winter in Africa and in summer fly to Europe to breed. Many Europeans think storks bring good luck. They build platforms on their chimneys so the birds can make their nests on them.

Find out more
Duck and Goose
Pelican
Swan

Flight

Things that fly need an upwards push, or force, to keep them in the air. This force is called lift. Without lift, another force, called gravity, pulls them back towards the ground. Aircraft, birds and insects all have wings. As they fly along, their wings use the air to make lift.

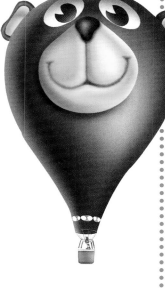

▷ Birds have strong muscles which make their wings flap up and down. Some birds, such as this seabird, have long, thin wings. They use them to glide as well as flap.

△ These balloons are full of hot air. Hot air is lighter than cold air, so the balloons are lighter than the air around them. This means they can float up into the air.

△ Some small aircraft have a propeller at the front. This is like a fan. It spins very fast, pushing air backwards and pulling the aircraft through the air.

◁ An aircraft's wings only make lift when the aircraft is speeding through the air. The air flows over and under the wing. Because of the wing's special curved shape, this makes lift.

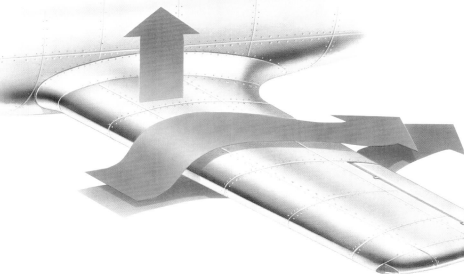

◁ Some seeds, such as these dandelion seeds, are very light and fluffy. They drift with the breeze until they reach a good place for growing.

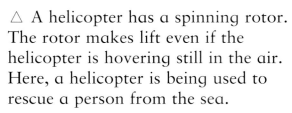

△ A helicopter has a spinning rotor. The rotor makes lift even if the helicopter is hovering still in the air. Here, a helicopter is being used to rescue a person from the sea.

◁ Blow hard on a dandelion seed-head. Watch the seeds. How long is it before they reach the ground?

Fact box
- A gnat flaps its wings a thousand times every second.
- The fastest aircraft in the world is the Lockheed SR-71A. It can fly at over 3,500 kilometres per hour.

◁ Put a piece of tissue paper on your bottom lip and blow gently to make air flow across the top of the paper. The tissue paper lifts up. A wing works in the same way. Its shape makes air flow faster over the top than the bottom.

Find out more
Air and Atmosphere
Engines
Floating
Force

Floating

Why do some things float in water and some things sink? Think about the space something takes up. This space is called its volume.

Things float if they weigh less than the same volume of water. A beach ball floats in water because it does not weigh as much as water with the same volume. A coin weighs more than water with the same volume, so it sinks.

△ These logs are floating down the river from the forest to the timber mill. They float well because wood is lighter than water.

▷ Test a few objects to see if they float. Then choose something that floats and try pushing it down into the water. Can you feel the water pushing it upwards? This upward push is called upthrust. Upthrust is the force that makes things float.

Fact box

• It's easier to float in salty water than in fresh water. The Dead Sea, between Israel and Jordan, is so salty that you can float without having to swim.

◁ A submarine can float or sink. To make it sink, water is let into tanks in the submarine's hull. This makes it heavier. To make it float again, air is pumped into the tanks to empty the water out. This makes it lighter.

Find out more
Flight
Force
Water

Flowers

Most plants have flowers. They are a very important part of a plant, because they make the seeds that grow into new plants. Many flowers have bright colours and a sweet smell to attract insects, such as bees and butterflies. The insects carry tiny grains of pollen from one flower to another so that seeds can be made.

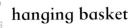
hanging basket

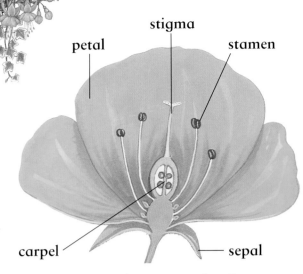

petal
stigma
stamen
carpel
sepal

△ These are the parts of a flower. Pollen is carried from the stamen of one flower to the stigma of another. This is called pollination.

pollen

▷ Flowers make nectar, which bees like to drink. As the bee drinks, pollen sticks to its body. When it flies to another flower, the pollen rubs off and pollinates it.

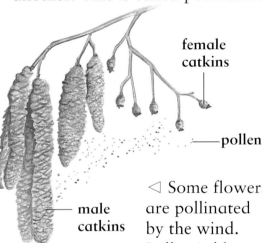

female catkins

pollen

male catkins

◁ Some flowers are pollinated by the wind. Pollen is blown from the male catkins to the female catkins.

1

2

3

4

△ **1** The flowers of a pear tree are pollinated by insects. **2** Tiny fruits start to grow under the flowers. The fruit protects the seeds inside.

△ **3** The fruits swell and grow. **4** When the fruits are fully grown they soften. Animals eat the fruit and spread the seeds.

Find out more
Conservation
Insects
Plants
Seasons
Water

118

Fly

There are many types of fly, and they are found everywhere. Unlike other insects, they have just one pair of wings for flying; their tiny back wings are only used for balance. A few flies carry deadly diseases, but many help plants by carrying pollen from one flower to another.

△ The African tsetse fly (pronounced 'tetsy') carries a disease called sleeping sickness. It spreads the disease from wild animals to humans and livestock by biting them and drinking their blood.

Fact box

• House-flies beat their wings 200 times a second.
• Midges beat their wings 1,000 times a second. It is this which makes the buzzing sound common to all flies.

△ The hover-fly, also called the flower-fly, gets its name from the fact that it hovers round flowers. Hover-flies have markings like wasps.

▽ Like all flies, dung-flies spend the first part of their lives as maggots. During this time, they live inside the dung left by animals. They feed on the dung and, in doing so, clear it up.

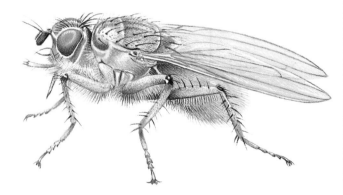

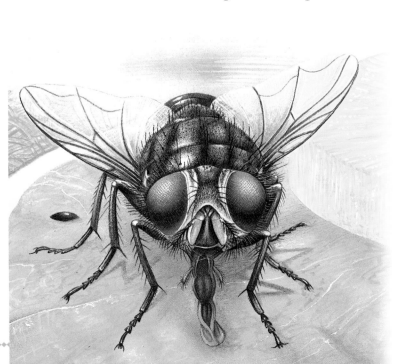

◁ Bluebottles (left) and house-flies feed on all kinds of food. They have 'taste buds' on their feet. These tell them whether something they have landed on is good to eat.

Find out more

Ant and Termite
Bee and Wasp
Beetle
Insect

Flying machines

There are all kinds of different flying machines, from hot-air balloons and gliders, to helicopters and passenger planes. The fastest way to travel is by aeroplane. An aeroplane has wings to lift it up into the air and an engine to push it forward. For hundreds of years people dreamed of being able to fly like a bird, but not until this century were they successful.

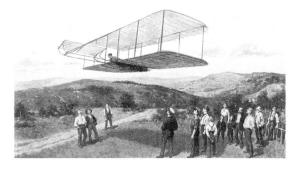

△ The first aeroplane was built by the Wright brothers over 90 years ago. The pilot had to lie on his stomach to fly it.

▷ This passenger jet can carry about 250 people. Jumbo jets are the largest passenger planes in the world. They can carry more than 400 people.

▽ This is a fighter plane. It is called a jump jet because it can take off straight up into the air. It can also hover above the ground.

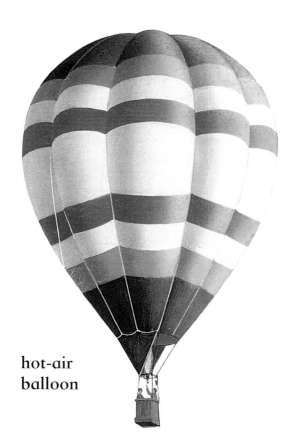

hot-air balloon

jump jet

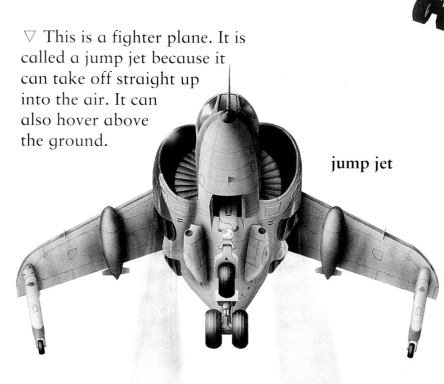

△ The air inside a hot-air balloon is heated by a powerful gas burner. Because hot air rises, it makes the balloon float up into the sky.

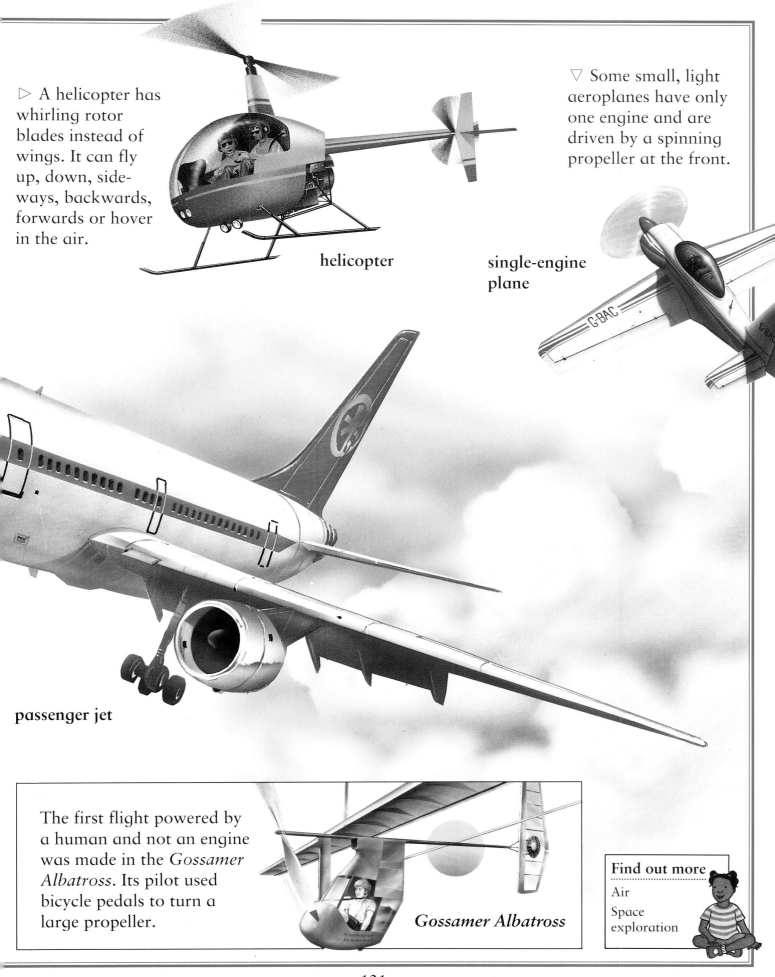

▷ A helicopter has whirling rotor blades instead of wings. It can fly up, down, sideways, backwards, forwards or hover in the air.

helicopter

▽ Some small, light aeroplanes have only one engine and are driven by a spinning propeller at the front.

single-engine plane

passenger jet

The first flight powered by a human and not an engine was made in the *Gossamer Albatross*. Its pilot used bicycle pedals to turn a large propeller.

Gossamer Albatross

Find out more

Air

Space exploration

Food

Food is important because it gives you energy to move and keep warm. It helps you to grow and to get better when you are ill. To stay healthy you need to eat lots of different kinds of food. You also need plenty of water to drink. Eating too many sugary or fatty foods is bad for your body.

proteins

△ Cheese, meat, eggs, nuts and fish give you proteins that build up your body and help it to stay strong.

▷ Fruit and vegetables have plenty of fibre. They help the food that you eat to pass through your body.

fibre

fats

△ Fats from foods like butter, milk, bacon, margarine and oil give you lots of energy. Your body can store extra fat to use later.

carbohydrates

△ Carbohydrates also give your body energy. Foods like bread, pasta, potatoes, noodles, beans and rice all have carbohydrates in them.

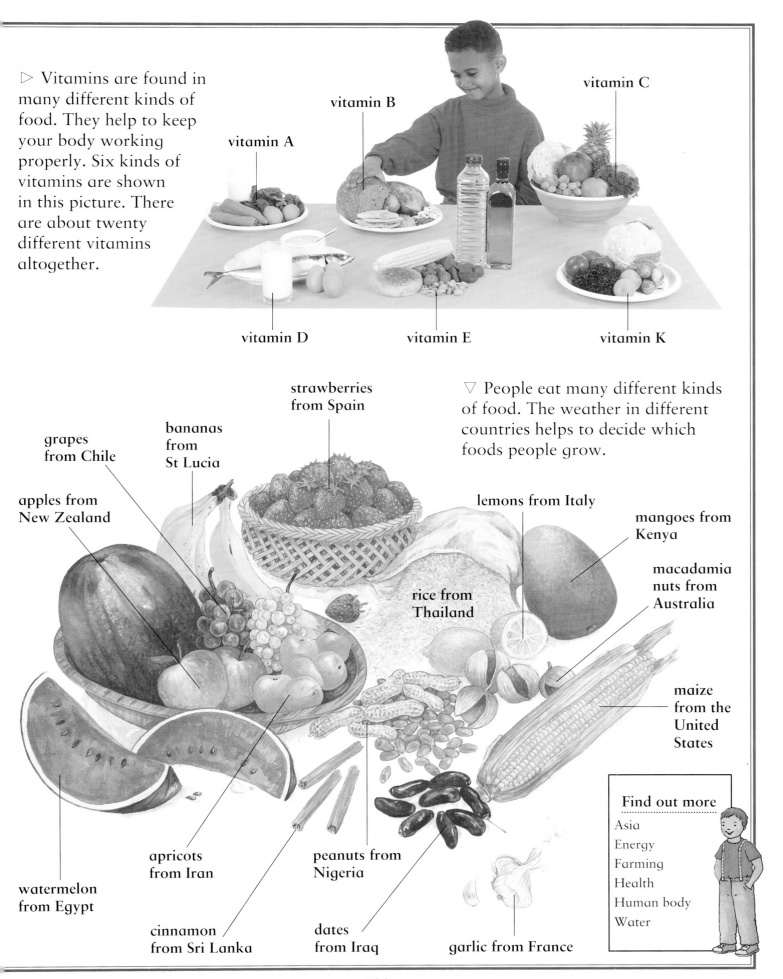

▷ Vitamins are found in many different kinds of food. They help to keep your body working properly. Six kinds of vitamins are shown in this picture. There are about twenty different vitamins altogether.

vitamin A

vitamin B

vitamin C

vitamin D

vitamin E

vitamin K

strawberries from Spain

▽ People eat many different kinds of food. The weather in different countries helps to decide which foods people grow.

grapes from Chile

bananas from St Lucia

apples from New Zealand

lemons from Italy

mangoes from Kenya

macadamia nuts from Australia

rice from Thailand

maize from the United States

watermelon from Egypt

apricots from Iran

peanuts from Nigeria

cinnamon from Sri Lanka

dates from Iraq

garlic from France

Find out more
Asia
Energy
Farming
Health
Human body
Water

Force

A force is a push or a pull. Forces can make things move. For example, to throw a ball, you push it hard to make it move quickly through the air. You also need a force to stop something moving. When you catch a ball, your hands push against it to slow it down. Engines and motors make forces that cause machines to move. The force of gravity pulls everything downwards towards the Earth.

△ This boy is pulling on the bar. He exerts a force that lifts him up. When he lets go, the force of gravity pulls him down to the ground.

▽ The force of gravity pulls this girl down the slide. Another force, called friction, slows her down slightly. But because the surface of the slide is smooth, she hardly notices. There is more friction if surfaces are rough.

◁ Forces can squash or stretch things. When this boy jumps on his pogo stick he squashes the ball under his feet. The ball then pushes him back upwards into the air.

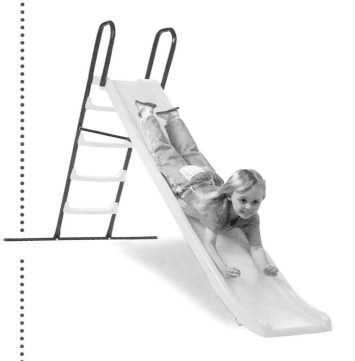

▷ These children are both exerting the same amount of force on the rope, but the forces are pulling in opposite directions. The two forces cancel each other out, so the rope does not move and nor do the children.

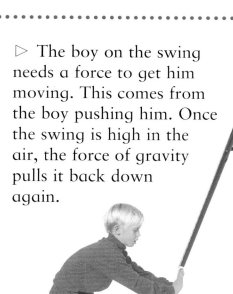

▷ The boy on the swing needs a force to get him moving. This comes from the boy pushing him. Once the swing is high in the air, the force of gravity pulls it back down again.

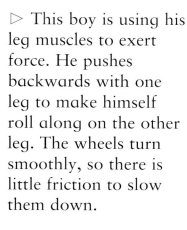

▷ This boy is using his leg muscles to exert force. He pushes backwards with one leg to make himself roll along on the other leg. The wheels turn smoothly, so there is little friction to slow them down.

▷ In these pictures, arrows show the direction the force is pushing or pulling. This girl is pushing as hard as she can.

△ It's much easier when two people push. The more force that is exerted on the sledge, the more quickly it will speed up.

Forests

Forests grow all over the world. The forest trees that grow in cold, dry parts of the world are very different from the trees that grow in warm, wet parts of the world.

A forest is home to many animals. The trees give them food and shelter them from the Sun, rain and wind.

△ Look at all these things. Wood from trees has been used to make them. Even the pages of this book are made from wood.

◁ Rainforests grow in hot, wet places. Over half of the world's animals and plants live in these forests. Huge areas of rainforest are cut down each year. This means that many of the animals and plants are in danger of dying out.

deciduous forests

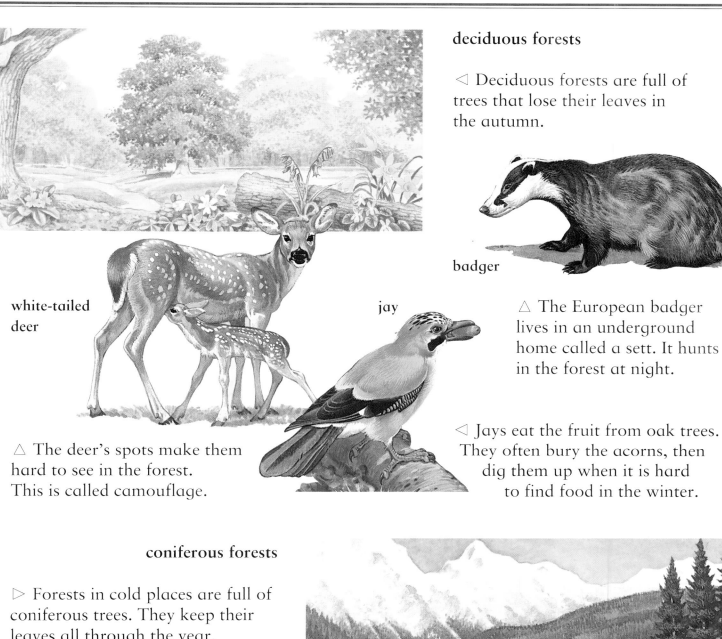

◁ Deciduous forests are full of trees that lose their leaves in the autumn.

badger

△ The European badger lives in an underground home called a sett. It hunts in the forest at night.

white-tailed deer

jay

△ The deer's spots make them hard to see in the forest. This is called camouflage.

◁ Jays eat the fruit from oak trees. They often bury the acorns, then dig them up when it is hard to find food in the winter.

coniferous forests

▷ Forests in cold places are full of coniferous trees. They keep their leaves all through the year.

moose

chipmunk

◁ A moose is a very large deer. It feeds on water plants and young tree shoots.

△ A chipmunk uses pouches in its cheeks to carry nuts and seeds back to its food store.

Find out more
Buildings
Conservation
Mountains
Trees
Trucks

Fossils

Fossils are the remains of plants and animals. Scientists study fossils of leaves, shells, footprints and skeletons to find out about life on Earth millions of years ago. When the plants and animals died, their remains were very slowly turned to stone.

▷ Nearly 200 years ago, 12-year-old Mary Anning found a huge fossil in a cliff. It was a sea creature called Plesiosaurus.

  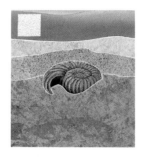 

△ **1** Ammonites lived in the sea millions of years ago. **2** When one died, its soft body rotted away. Layers of mud buried its hard shell.

△ **3** Very slowly, over thousands of years, the mud turned to rock and the shell became a fossil. **4** Many years later the fossil was dug up.

spider in amber

△ This spider has been kept whole in a piece of amber. Amber is sticky tree sap which has turned hard.

▷ This Woolly mammoth was frozen for thousands of years in the icy ground of Siberia, in Russia.

Woolly mammoth

◁ Fossils of plants are often found in large lumps of coal. This is a type of fern.

Find out more
Dinosaurs
Prehistoric life

Fox

Foxes are small wild dogs with short legs and big, bushy tails. They are skilful hunters that come out at night and rest by day in burrows called dens. The female is called a vixen, the male is a dog and the young are cubs.

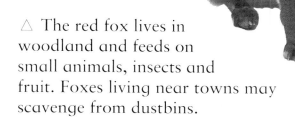

good hearing

sharp eyesight

excellent sense of smell

△ The red fox lives in woodland and feeds on small animals, insects and fruit. Foxes living near towns may scavenge from dustbins.

◁ Foxes are found in most parts of the world. The fennec fox lives in the deserts of North Africa and Arabia. During the day it stays below ground in its burrow to avoid the heat of the sun. Its huge ears also help it to lose heat and to keep cool.

▷ Foxes' pointed ears give them very good hearing. This helps them detect the slightest noise of a small animal in the grass. Roll two pieces of card into cones and hold them to your ears. Get a friend to make a noise behind you, then hear for yourself the difference with the cones and without.

Find out more
Dog (domestic)
Dog (wild)

Friction

Friction is a force which tries to stop one surface sliding against another. There is more friction between rough surfaces than between smooth surfaces. Friction stops your feet sliding on the ground as you walk. It stops things slipping from your grasp, and stops bicycle tyres skidding when you brake. Look out for friction at home or at school.

△ Find out how different surfaces are affected by friction. Slide different objects down a slope. Try coins, pens and pencils, and a rubber. Which ones slide most easily?

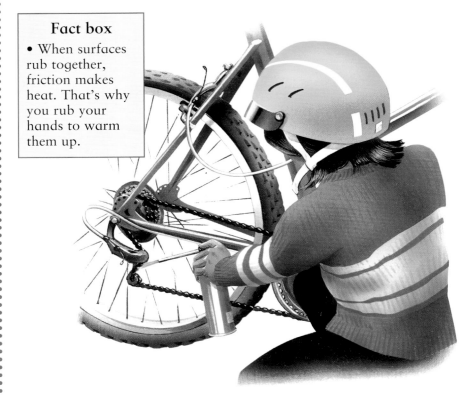

◁ This girl is putting oil on her bicycle gears and chain. The oil reduces friction. It lets the gear wheels turn more easily and makes the chain more flexible. This makes pedalling easier and stops the gears wearing out. Oil also stops the metal parts going rusty.

◁ Friction also tries to slow down things that are moving through the air. There is less air friction on things with a smooth, streamlined shape, such as this sporty car.

Find out more
Air and Atmosphere
Force
Machines
Water

Frog and Toad

Frogs and toads are amphibians so they live both in water and on land. Frogs have moist skins but toads are normally dry. While frogs use their strong back legs for jumping, toads walk. They are both good swimmers.

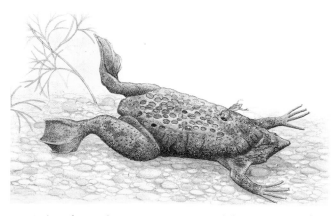

△ The female Surinam toad has special pockets on her back in which her eggs grow. After 80 days, the young toads emerge from the pockets.

△ Many tropical frogs are brightly coloured. This warns other animals that they are poisonous. The poison of the South American poison dart frog (bottom) is so strong that native people put it on the tips of their arrows.

▷ **1** Most frogs and toads lay their eggs, called spawn, in water. **2** After two weeks, tadpoles hatch. **3** Like fish, they breathe through gills, but gradually grow legs. **4** After three months, the gills shrink, the tail gets short and the lungs develop. **5, 6** The tiny frogs are able to leave the water and grow into adults on land.

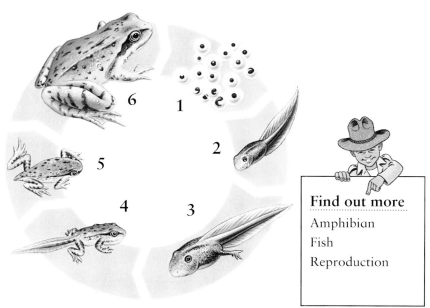

Find out more
Amphibian
Fish
Reproduction

Fuels

Fuels are sources of energy. We need energy for heating, cooking, lighting and to make machines work. This energy comes from fuels. When fuels burn, they release energy. Some fuels, such as coal, oil and gas are found under the ground. Food is also a fuel. Animals eat food to get energy to live.

△ Food is fuel for your body. It provides you with the energy you need to move – or even just to sit and think.

◁ The engines in cars and other vehicles make dirty waste gases when they burn fuel. These gases float into the air, making it dirty and harmful to people, other animals and plants. This dirtiness is called pollution. Modern cars have special parts that cut down the amount of pollution they make.

▷ Power stations make electricity for our homes, offices and factories. Most use fossil fuels – coal, oil and gas. Every day, hundreds of tonnes of coal are burned at this power station. This makes heat energy, which is turned into movement energy, and then into electrical energy.

◁ Oil is often found deep under the sea bed. To get it out, a deep hole has to be drilled. Then, the oil is pumped up through long pipes. Oil is used to make petrol, diesel and other kinds of fuel.

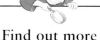

Find out more
Earth
Electricity
Energy
Living things
Machines
Materials
Nuclear energy

Gases

Everything that exists is a solid, a liquid or a gas. These are called the states of matter. Gases are different from other states. They spread out to fill the space they are in. They can also be squeezed into a smaller space. You cannot squeeze a liquid or a solid.

Most gases are invisible. But some have a strong smell, so you know they are there.

△ Try making a gas and watch it fill a balloon. You need vinegar, a bottle, some bicarbonate of soda, a balloon and a funnel.

1

△ **1** Pour some vinegar into the bottle, until it is about 5 cm deep. Now pour some soda into the balloon. Use the funnel for this.

2

△ **2** Fit the neck of the balloon over the top of the bottle. Then shake the balloon so that the soda drops into the bottle.

3

△ **3** The soda and the vinegar fizz and give off bubbles of carbon dioxide gas. The gas fills the bottle and blows up the balloon.

◁ The molecules, or tiny particles, that make up a gas have a lot of space between them. Gases can be squeezed into a smaller space by pushing the molecules closer together.

Find out more
Air and Atmosphere
Chemistry and Chemicals
Solids

133

Giraffe

Giraffes are the world's tallest animals, measuring up to six metres. Their front legs are so long that they have to spread them wide apart in order to drink at water holes.

▽ Giraffes live in small family groups on the African plains. About 15 months after mating the female giraffe gives birth to a calf. The calf can get onto its feet and follow its mother only an hour or two after being born.

◁ The spotted pattern on its coat helps to hide the giraffe from its enemies. Spots can be big (above), or blotchy (left). Each giraffe has a different pattern.

△ Giraffes use their height to graze on the leaves at the top of acacia thorn trees. The giraffe tears off the spiky twigs in its tough mouth. It can also curl its long tongue round even higher branches and pull them down to its mouth.

Find out more
Antelope
Zebra

Goat

Hardy and good at climbing, goats can survive in the highest mountains. Wild goats are found across the Northern Hemisphere. Tame goats are kept for their milk, meat and skin.

feral goat

Cretan wild goat

Apennine mountain goat

△ Kashmir and Angora goats are valued for their fine wool. The long, silky coat of the Angora (above) gives mohair or angora wool. Kashmir goats give cashmere wool.

Fact box

• Goats' hooves have hard edges and soft centres. They act like suckers on steep, slippery rocks.
• Goats give off a very strong smell.
• A young goat is a called a kid, a female is a doe or a nanny, and a male is a billy.

△ Goats were first tamed 10,000 years ago, and there are now many breeds. They like to eat grass and plants, but they will eat almost anything and can survive on thorn trees and shrubs. Male goats are often bad-tempered and use their long, curved horns to fight each other for females.

▽ Ibexes are wild goats found in Europe, Africa and Asia. They live on the mountaintops in summer, and move to warmer, lower pastures in winter.

Find out more

Antelope
Cow and Bull
Yak

Goldfish and Carp

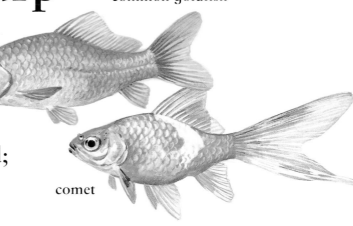

common goldfish

comet

Goldfish and carp originally came from lakes and streams in Asia and were first brought to Europe by the Romans. Goldfish are often small and brightly coloured; carp are larger and usually have plainer colouring.

△ Goldfish survive well in both outdoor ponds and tanks indoors. They come in a wide range of colours and shapes.

silver carp

△ 1 Looking after goldfish is easy. You will need a tank with clean gravel and a few large objects. You should also put in some water plants to give the fish oxygen to breathe.

▷ 2 Fill the tank with water and carefully place the goldfish in the tank. You will need to feed them daily and you must be sure to clean the tank and change the water regularly.

△ Carp can now be found in North America as well as Europe. Grass carp are helpful to humans because they eat pondweed. In China, the silver carp is bred for food.

Find out more
Eel
Fish
Salmon and Trout

Gorilla

Gorillas are huge and powerful apes. They look fierce, but are actually gentle vegetarians. They are now very rare and are found only in the forests and mountains of Central Africa.

▽ Gorillas live in family groups. These are led by a big male called a silverback, who gets his name from the silver hairs on his back. These hairs grow when a male gorilla is about ten years old. Silverbacks may be as tall as a man and weigh 225 kilograms – about three times as much as a man.

△ Gorillas eat leaves and buds, stalks, berries and sometimes even tree bark. When they have eaten most of the food in one place, they move on to let the plants grow back again.

◁▽ Gorillas learn to walk at about ten months. They feed on their mother's milk for the first two years and spend much of their time playing. They sleep with their mothers until they are three years old, then they make their own nests of leaves and branches.

Find out more
Baboon
Chimpanzee
Monkey
Orang-utan

Grasslands

Grasslands cover huge areas of the world. They are sometimes too dry for many trees to grow. Grasses are tough plants that grow quickly.

The hot grassland of Africa is called savanna and in Australia it is called the bush. Grasslands are called pampas in South America, prairies in North America and steppes in Asia.

△ In Australia the bush often catches fire in the dry season. Grass grows well in the ash-rich soil.

▽ The African savanna often looks brown and dry. In the short rainy season it is fresh and green.

△ Huge areas of the prairies of North America are used to grow wheat.

pampas grass

◁ This type of grass grows on the pampas of South America. It has long, fluffy flowers.

Find out more
Africa
Asia
Camouflage
Farming
North America
South America

138

Guinea pig, Gerbil and Hamster

Guinea pigs, gerbils and hamsters are all mammals. These rodents live wild in many parts of the world, but they also make very good pets. They need a good-sized cage and should be given food and water every day. They also enjoy lots of care and attention.

▽ In South America, humans have been eating guinea pig meat for about 4,000 years. Wild guinea pigs, called cavies, still live on the grasslands there.

△ Guinea pigs feed on grass and green plants in the wild, so if you give them dry pet food, make sure they have plenty of water.

▽ Hamsters live alone and come out at night to eat grasses, seeds and berries. They have big pouches in their cheeks that they use to carry food back to their nests.

▷ Gerbils live on the edges of hot deserts. They hide in burrows by day and come out at night to feed on seeds and insects. Their long back legs and tails help them to leap across the hot, sandy ground.

Find out more
Beaver
Mouse
Rabbit and Hare
Rat
Squirrel

Gull

Gulls, or seagulls, are large, sturdy sea birds with webbed feet. There are over 40 species, found in coastal areas all over the world. Sometimes gulls are found inland, in the countryside and in towns and cities.

△ Gulls eat many different foods, including fish, eggs, earthworms and insects. They also scavenge for food on rubbish dumps.

▽ Baby gulls are covered in soft, fluffy feathers, called down. They are fed by their parents until the chicks have grown their flight feathers.

▽ Gulls are strong fliers, soaring and gliding on the strong sea breezes. Many gulls nest on cliffs, forming large and noisy colonies.

▽ Parents often have to fend off other gulls, like the lesser black-backed gull, that try to eat eggs and chicks from their nests.

Find out more
Albatross
Bird
Duck and Goose
Sea bird

Habitat

A habitat is the place where an animal lives. It provides the animal with food, water and shelter – everything it needs to survive. There are many different habitats all over the world.

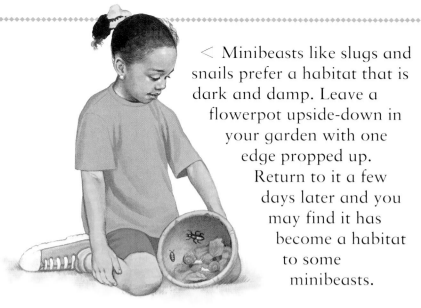

< Minibeasts like slugs and snails prefer a habitat that is dark and damp. Leave a flowerpot upside-down in your garden with one edge propped up. Return to it a few days later and you may find it has become a habitat to some minibeasts.

savanna

rainforest

desert

△ Over time, animals have evolved to survive in their own habitats. For example, the camel is able to live in the desert because it can go for days without drinking. If a habitat changes – for example, if the rainfall decreases – each animal must adapt to the new environment. Unlike humans, if an animal is suddenly taken out of its habitat it cannot adapt quickly enough and is unlikely to survive.

Find out more

Camel
Chimpanzee
Evolution
Giraffe

Health

You need to be healthy to keep your body working properly. A healthy diet gives your body fuel and helps it to grow and repair itself. Keeping clean helps to stop the germs that can cause illness spreading. Exercise helps your body to grow strong. Caring for yourself will keep you fit and healthy.

△ You need different foods to keep you strong and healthy. Eating a variety of foods and drinking lots of water gives you energy and helps you grow.

◁ Playing football and other games is a good way to take exercise. Exercise makes your muscles strong and keeps your body fit.

▽ Washing with soap and water keeps your skin clean. Keeping clean stops illnesses and germs spreading.

Fact box

• The outside of your teeth is covered with hard enamel. Fizzy drinks and sweets eat this away.

• People are given injections, called vaccinations, to prevent them catching nasty illnesses.

• Most children sleep for about 12 hours every night.

▷ If you graze your skin, it should be cleaned so that germs cannot get in. Germs are tiny living things. Some of them can make you ill.

▽ Your body needs sleep to give your brain and muscles time to rest. When you are asleep, your body also has time to grow.

▷ Dentists look after teeth. If they find a hole, they make a filling. Don't eat too many sweets and brush your teeth every day to keep them clean.

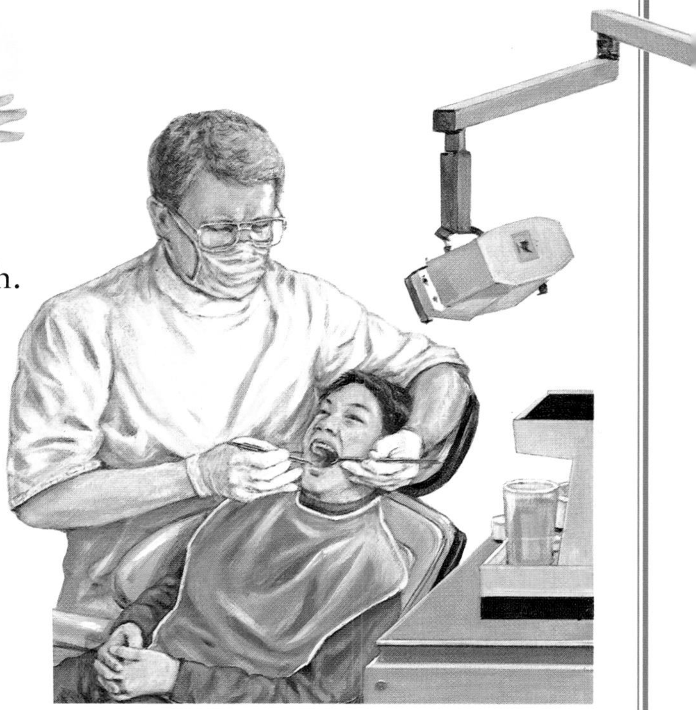

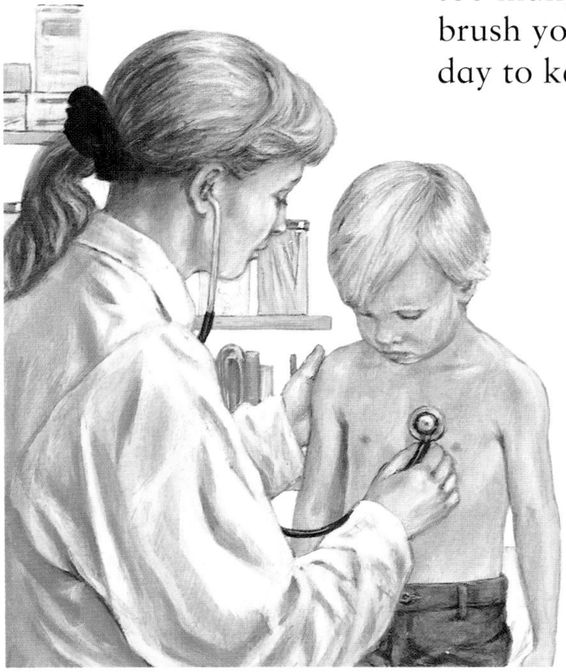

◁ Doctors look after you when you are ill. They may listen to your heart or look down your throat. If you need any medicine, they will give you this to help you get better.

Find out more
Conservation
Food
Human body
Sports
Water

Hedgehog

Hedgehogs are mammals found in the woods and hedges of Europe, Asia and Africa. Most have thousands of thick spines covering their backs, which help to protect them from predators. There are also hairy hedgehogs, which live in Asia.

▽ The common hedgehog usually has about four babies. The babies do not get pricked when they drink their mother's milk as she only has spines on her back. Adults go out after dark to hunt for food. They will eat plants, but prefer insects and frogs.

Fact box
• Babies are born blind, with soft spines.
• Hedgehogs spend more than 20 hours a day sleeping. In cold northern regions, they hibernate in winter, curling up under a pile of leaves.
• One hedgehog, the moon rat of Sumatra, can be 40cm long.

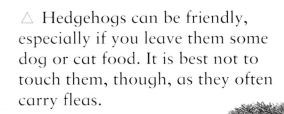

△ Hedgehogs can be friendly, especially if you leave them some dog or cat food. It is best not to touch them, though, as they often carry fleas.

△ When a hedgehog senses danger, it curls up into a tight ball with its spines on the outside. This puts off most predators, although many hedgehogs are killed by cars when they curl up on roads. They are able to climb trees and, if they fall, the spines act as a cushion.

Find out more
Fox
Mole

Hippopotamus

These huge animals have large barrel-shaped bodies and short legs. The name hippopotamus comes from Greek and means 'river horse'. Although they are not related to horses, they do live near rivers – in Africa.

▷ Hippos spend the day in the water with just their eyes, nose and ears showing. This stops them getting sunburnt. They can stay underwater for up to ten minutes before having to come up for air.

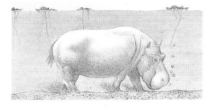

Fact box

• Hippos live in groups of up to 15 in rivers, lakes and ponds across Africa.
• They can grow to 4.6 metres long, stand 1.5 metres at the shoulder and weigh as much as 4.5 tonnes.
• Hippos are related to pigs.

△ Hippos have gigantic mouths with two huge tusks on the bottom jaw. In the breeding season, competing males show off the size of their mouths and may cut each other with their tusks. Hippos leave the water at night and travel to look for the grasses they eat. They have hard lips, which they use to cut the grass.

◁ Baby hippos can weigh 55 kilograms at birth. They can stand within minutes of being born, and must keep close to their mother for protection.

Find out more
Horse
Pig
Rhinoceros

History

History is the study of what happened in the past. Historians read old books, papers and manuscripts to discover the facts. They look for clues in paintings, old buildings, maps and photographs. Archaeologists study the things people made and used. They try to find ruined buildings and buried objects, such as tools, weapons and pots. These help to show how people lived long ago.

△ Older people can tell you about events and daily life when they were young. Their childhood was probably very different from yours.

◁ Archaeologists often dig in the ground or search underwater to find clues about houses, tombs, bones and many everyday objects.

▷ Reading books on history is a good way to find out about the past. Television and radio have history programmes too.

△ Museums display objects from all over the world for people to come and see. Museums help all of us to learn more about the past.

Ancient Egypt

Some Egyptian pharaohs were buried in pyramids. Their bodies were rowed down the Nile River and sealed inside a tomb filled with food, weapons and furniture.

△ People visit ancient sites like the pyramids to find out more about history. Paintings on the walls inside tell us how the Egyptians once lived.

Ancient Greece

The Greeks performed plays in open-air theatres. They had a circular floor for dancing with a stage behind. All the parts were played by men who wore masks.

△ The ruins of many Greek theatres are still standing. These tell us how the theatres looked.

Ancient China
The Great Wall of China is the longest wall ever built. It was built to keep out enemy tribes. The wall had towers for look-out posts.

▷ Some of the Great Wall of China still stands today. People like to walk along its top.

Ancient Americas
The Aztecs ruled a mighty empire in what is now Mexico. They were fierce warriors. They built pyramids with temples on top to make offerings to their gods.

△ Aztec men wore brooches like this one made of gold and turquoise to fasten their cloaks.

Second World War

Many cities, like Cologne in Germany, were bombed in the Second World War. The war lasted for five years and many millions of people died.

▷ After the war, the buildings in Cologne were quickly rebuilt. This picture shows how it looks today.

◁ No one knows who carved these enormous stone heads on Easter Island in the Pacific Ocean. We are still learning about the past but some things may always stay a mystery.

Find out more

Art and artists
Books
Castles

Horse

Long legs, a big heart and large lungs make horses strong and fast – which is why people have used them to ride and to pull carts for 5,000 years. Horses are descended from wild horses that once lived on grassy plains in herds.

▷ Horses come in many colours, each with a special name.

dun
dark bay
roan
light bay
palomino
piebald
chestnut
skewbald
grey
black

◁ Ponies can be kept as family pets. They need a field to live in, and lots of care and attention. They should be exercised regularly and need their hooves trimmed every few weeks.

▽ Grooming keeps a pony's coat glossy and healthy. Be sure never to walk behind a horse or pony – it may kick out in surprise.

▽ Every part, or point, of a horse has a name. Horses are measured in hands. One hand is four inches (about ten centimetres) – the width of a man's hand.

forelock
mane
withers
hindquarters
tail
shoulder
hock
fetlock
hoof

Find out more
Donkey
Evolution
Mammal
Zebra

Human body

Your body is like a complicated machine. Inside and out, it is made up of lots of different working parts. How many do you know? Each of these parts has a job to do. For example, you think with your brain, you chew with your teeth and you see with your eyes. All these parts work together to keep you alive.

▽ Inside your body, there is a framework of bones, called your skeleton. This supports your body and protects the parts inside it.

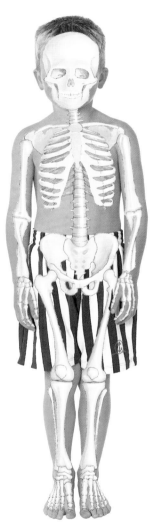

▷ There are millions of tiny cells in your body. They make up every part of you. This is what a muscle cell looks like when you see it through a microscope.

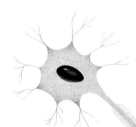

nerve cell

muscle cell

skin cell

△ Nerve cells are also called neurons. They carry messages between your brain and your body. Some nerve cells are very long. The nerve cells that run down your leg to your toes can be over a metre long.

△ Different cells have different shapes and sizes. This is what one of your skin cells looks like.

▽ Everyone's body works the same way, but no one else looks quite like you!

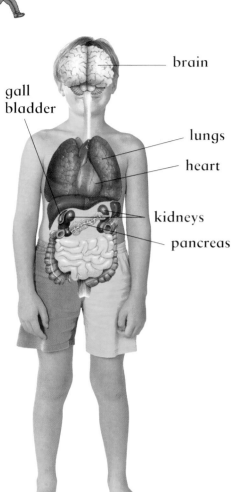

brain

gall
bladder

lungs

heart

kidneys

pancreas

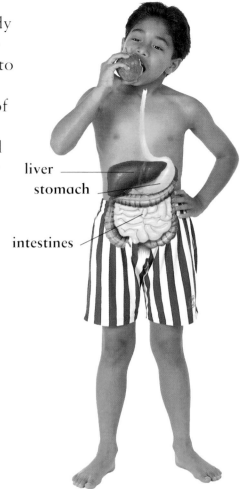

liver

stomach

intestines

▷ Some organs are joined up into systems. Food travels through your body along your digestive system. Here it is broken into tiny bits and mixed with chemicals. Useful parts of the food pass into your blood and are carried all around your body. Your cells need energy from food to work.

◁ Some parts of your body are called organs. Each one has a job to do. Your heart pumps blood around your body. Your lungs help you breathe, and your stomach helps you digest your food. Your brain lets you think and controls the rest of your body.

▷ Like everything else inside you, blood is made up of cells. There are two kinds of blood cells – red and white. The red cells get their colour from a chemical inside them. It carries oxygen from the air you breathe in. All your cells need oxygen to stay alive. White cells help you fight disease. Blood travels around your body along tiny tubes called blood vessels.

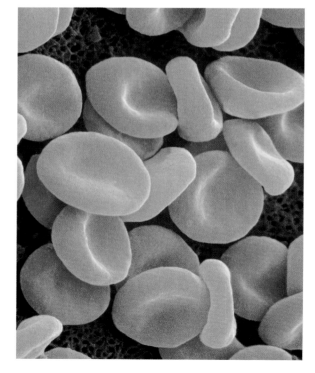

▷ Your heart pumps blood to parts of your body along arteries (coloured blue). The blood goes back to your heart along veins (coloured red). Then it is pumped to your lungs, and then back around your body again.

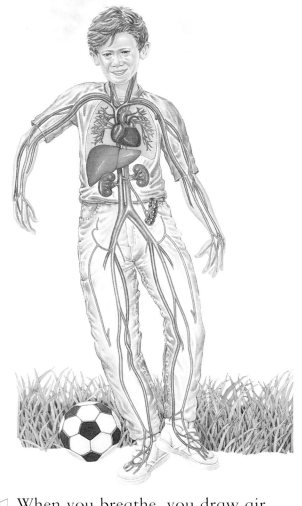

△ When you move, your muscles and bones work together. The muscles in your arm pull on the bones to make your arm bend and straighten.

◁ When you breathe, you draw air down your windpipe into your lungs. Oxygen from the air goes from your lungs into your blood and is carried to all the cells in your body. They need oxygen to stay alive.

◁ Your heart pumps blood around your body. It pumps, or beats, about once every second. Press gently on a friend's wrist. Can you feel it throb as blood surges through the blood vessel there?

Hummingbird

When hummingbirds hover, their wings beat so fast that they hum, and this gives them their name. These tiny birds live in warm places in North and South America.

▽ Hummingbirds use their long beaks to reach the nectar deep inside flowers.

◁ Hummingbirds use up so much energy beating their wings that they need to feed often. The nectar they eat is full of sugar, which gives them energy quickly.

△ A hummingbird's wings swivel. This means it can hover at a flower while keeping its head perfectly still. It can also fly backwards.

Fact box

• Ruby-throated hummingbirds fly 800km nonstop across the Gulf of Mexico when migrating.
• Hummingbirds normally lay two eggs, which are the smallest of any bird's.
• There are over 300 species of hummingbird.

▷ All hummingbirds are tiny, but the bee hummingbird of Cuba is the world's smallest bird. It is just 5.5 centimetres long – no bigger than a child's thumb.

Find out more
Bird
Migration
Ostrich

Hyena

Hyenas are mammals that live in Africa and Asia. They mainly eat the bones and flesh left by lions after a kill. Their jaws are so strong that they can crush and eat bones that even lions cannot manage.

striped hyena

brown hyena

△ Brown and striped hyenas are smaller and less fierce than spotted hyenas. They often prowl around at night, eating the remains of other animals' kills.

▷ Spotted hyenas are also known as laughing hyenas because of the weird cries they make. The largest and strongest of hyenas, they grow up to two metres long. Spotted hyenas hunt in packs and sometimes they will attack rhinos.

◁ The aardwolf is a close relative of the hyena that lives in southern Africa. It is smaller than a hyena and eats only termites, ants and insects.

Find out more
Dog (wild)
Fox
Lion

Insects

Insects are animals with six legs. Most insects are tiny and have wings. Even the largest insect, the goliath beetle, is only ten centimetres long. Many insects are brightly coloured and some look like leaves or twigs to help them hide from their enemies.

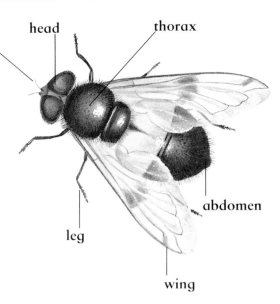

feeler

head

thorax

abdomen

leg

wing

 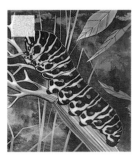 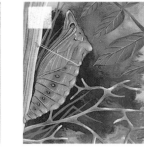 

adult swallowtail butterfly

△ 1 A female butterfly lays eggs on a plant that her young will eat. Each egg hatches into a caterpillar. 2 A caterpillar eats greedily and grows quickly.

△ 3 The caterpillar turns into a chrysalis. 4 The adult butterfly bursts out of the chrysalis.

potter wasp

< A female potter wasp makes a clay pot for each of her eggs. She puts live caterpillars in each pot, so the baby wasp has food when it hatches.

△ The dragonfly is the fastest insect. It flies above ponds and streams hunting for other insects to eat.

bumble bee

cockroach

◁ Bees collect nectar and pollen from flowers. They take this to their nests to feed their grubs.

▷ Cockroaches are unpleasant insects. They spoil our food and they often carry germs.

Fact Box

• An insect's body has three parts – the head, thorax and abdomen.

• Feelers are used to smell and feel.

• Some insects can taste with their feet.

• Most insects are less than six millimetres long.

• Ants live in big groups called colonies.

leaf-cutter ants

△ Leaf-cutter ants can lift leaves that are larger than themselves. They carry the leaves back to their nests.

◁ This is the actual size of an adult goliath beetle. It can weigh as much as a mouse.

mosquito

goliath beetle

Find out more

Animals
Camouflage
Colour
Europe
Farming
Flowers
Health
Light
Water

▷ A female mosquito sucks human and animal blood. It uses its sharp mouthparts to pierce the skin and suck up the blood through a tube.

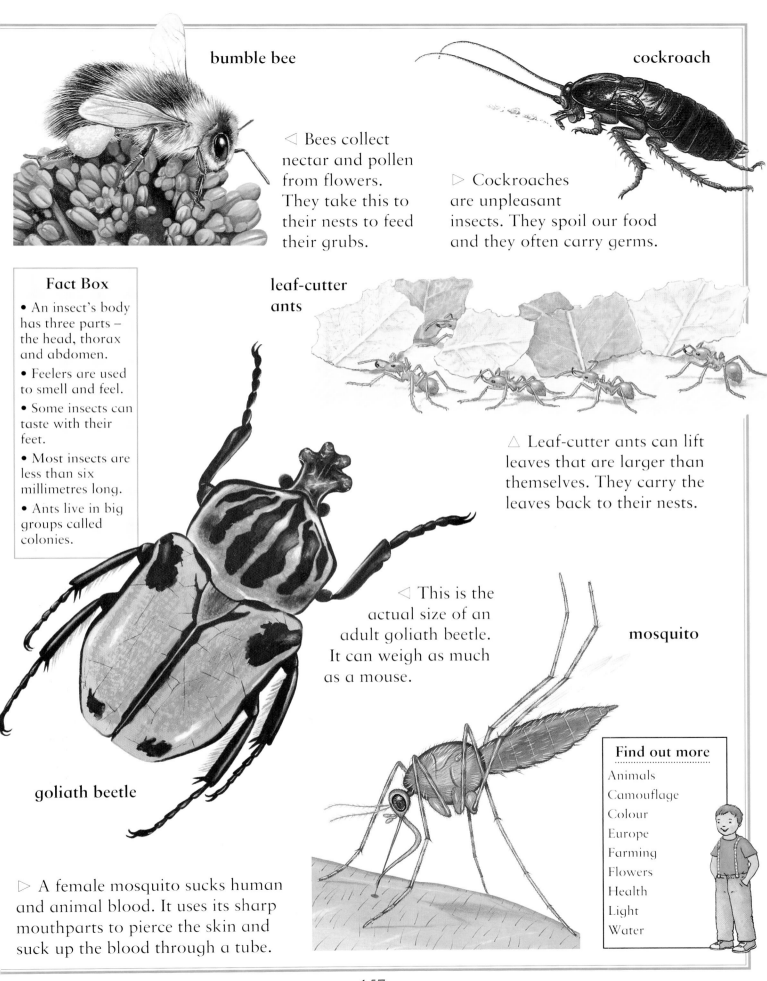

Inventions

Inventions are new ways of doing things. Some have made life more comfortable or have improved our health. Some have helped us to travel further and faster. Some have changed how we talk to one another. But not all inventions have been for the good. Guns and bombs have changed the way wars are fought.

△ Long ago, people discovered it was easier to roll heavy things. Then they invented the wheel.

wheel

fridge

▽ Plastic is made from chemicals in factories. It is a useful invention because it is easy to shape and it is tough. Lots of things are plastic.

△ A fridge keeps food and drink cool. Cool food stays fresher for longer. Before fridges were invented, people kept food cool with large blocks of frozen ice.

▷ Television brings pictures and sounds from all over the world into our homes. We watch the TV to learn and to relax.

television

▽ An incubator is a warm, closed cot. It protects sick babies and ones that are born too early. They stay there until they are strong and well.

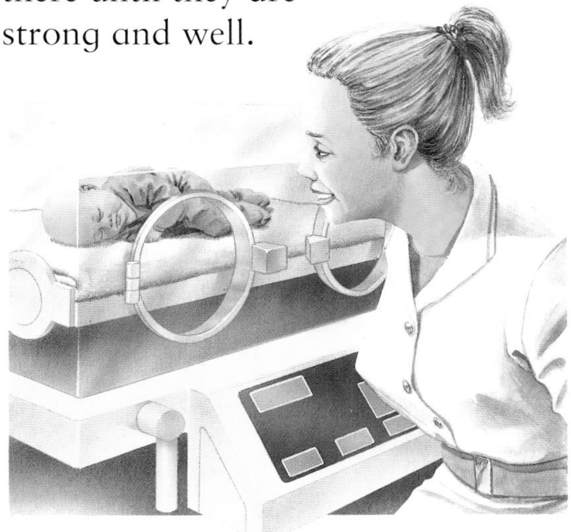

incubator

▷ This is a very old telescope. It was built by Galileo, a famous astronomer. He used it to look at the Moon and the planets.

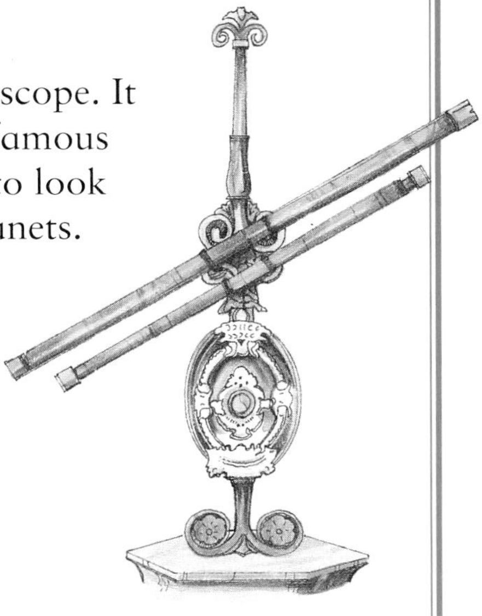

telescope

▽ Using a camera to take photographs is an easy way to keep a record of people, places and events you have seen.

▽ The invention of the telephone makes it possible for you to talk to someone else almost anywhere in the world.

camera

telephone

Find out more

Bikes
Books
Cars
Computers
Flying machines
Trains
Space exploration

Jobs

People do all sorts of jobs. They may farm or fish. They may make things in a factory or sell things in a shop. They may build homes, drive trucks or look after ill people. People work to earn money. They may start jobs when they leave school or college and stop work when they get old.

△ Teachers work in schools. They help children to learn the things they need to know.

△ Farming is an important job all over the world. This man is cutting sugar cane.

△ Many people work in offices. They use computers and telephones to help them.

△ Supermarkets provide jobs. This man is arranging food on the shelves.

▷ These people are making a film. Each has a different job, such as acting, directing, recording the sound and filming.

Find out more

Books
Computers
Farming

Kangaroo and Wallaby

Kangaroos and wallabies live in Australia. They are marsupials. This means that the females have pouches on their bellies where their babies can grow until they are big enough to come out into the world.

▷ A baby kangaroo is called a joey. When it is born, the baby is just two centimetres long. It crawls up to the mother's pouch along a path the mother licks in her fur. Once in the pouch, the joey clings to a teat and stays there until it is able to look after itself.

△ There are 56 species of kangaroo and wallaby (the name given to the smaller kangaroos). Most live on the ground, but some live in trees.

▷ Kangaroos are brilliant jumpers. They bound along on their strong back legs, using their long tails for balance. They can jump over ten metres in one leap.

Find out more
Koala, Wombat and Opossum
Mammal
Platypus

Killer whale

Killer whales are the largest members of the dolphin family. They are powerful hunters and can be up to ten metres in length. Killer whales have strong jaws and teeth. They eat fish, dolphins, seals – even other whales.

▽ Killer whales find their way and track their prey by sending out little clicks of sound, then picking up the echo. They live in families called pods. Usually there are ten or so in a pod, but there may be up to 100. Like all whales, killer whales are mammals and give birth to live young.

Fact box
• Killer whales sometimes launch themselves onto a beach to catch seals resting near to the water line.
• One killer whale caught in the Bering Sea had 32 seals in its stomach.
• Killer whales have never killed, or even attacked, humans.

△ Killer whales are fast swimmers, with rounded flippers and strong tails. They can swim at over 55 kilometres per hour, and can jump high out of the water. They live in most of the world's oceans, near the North and South Poles.

Find out more
Dolphin
Shark

Koala, Wombat and Opossum

Koalas live in the eucalyptus forests of eastern Australia. Because they look a little like bears, they are sometimes called koala bears. However, they are marsupials, not bears. Wombats and opossums are also marsupials.

△ Wombats look like koalas, and also live in Australia. But they are larger – between 70 and 120 centimetres long – and live on the ground. During the day they stay in the grassy nests that they make at the end of their long burrows. They come out at night to feed on grasses and the roots of shrubs and trees.

▽ The only marsupials to live outside Australia are opossums, which are found in North and South America. A typical opossum grows to about 100 centimetres long. At least half its length is its hairless tail, which can grip things.

△ When a young koala leaves its mother's pouch, it rides on her back. Koalas spend all their lives up in eucalyptus trees eating the leaves and bark. They only come down to cross to another clump of trees.

Find out more

Kangaroo and Wallaby
Mammal
Platypus

Light and Lenses

Without light we could not see anything. During the day, most of the light we see comes from the Sun. At night, we have artifical lights inside our homes and on the streets outside. Light usually travels in straight lines called rays. We see things because the rays hit an object, then bounce back into our eyes.

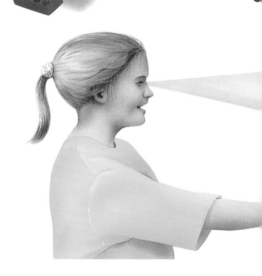

▷ Light from the Sun and light bulbs is called white light. It is made up of different colours mixed together. Things look coloured because they only reflect (bounce back) some of these colours and not others.

◁ Light travels in straight lines called rays. If the rays cannot reach a surface because there is something stopping them, a shadow forms. Your hand makes a shadow on the wall because it is stopping the light reaching the wall.

▷ Light rays can be bent or made to change direction. When you put a straw in a glass, it looks bent. This is because the rays of light reflected from the straw bend when they leave the water and pass into the air.

Fact box
• Light travels at 300,000 kilometres per second. It takes eight minutes for rays of sunlight to get from the Sun to the Earth.

▽ This desert traveller can see a welcome pool of water in front of the palm trees. But the water is not really there. This is called a mirage. It happens when layers of warm air near the ground bend rays of light from the bright sky.

△ Like sunlight, the light from this torch is a mix of many colours. When the girl shines the torch on the green balloon, the balloon soaks up all the colours in the light, except green. Green light bounces back into the girl's eyes and she sees a green balloon.

◁ Some creatures, such as this glow-worm, can produce light from their own bodies. The light is not to help the glow-worm see. It is to attract a mate.

◁ A magnifying glass makes things look bigger. It does this by bending the straight rays of light as they pass through the glass lens.

▽ A telescope makes objects in the distance look larger. If you point a telescope at the night sky, you can see many more stars than you can with your eyes alone. This is because the telescope collects lots more light than your eyes can collect.

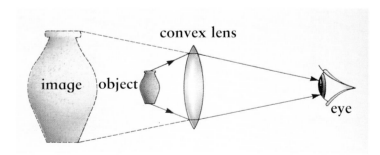

△ A magnifying glass works like this. When rays of light pass through the lens, they are bent inwards, towards each other. When they reach your eye they seem to be coming from a much larger object.

convex lens

concave lens

△ A lens that bulges in the middle is called a convex lens. When rays of light pass through it, they bend inwards, towards each other. A magnifying glass has a convex lens.

▽ A lens that is thinner in the middle is called a concave lens. Rays of light passing through it spread outwards. If you look at something through a concave lens, it often looks smaller than it really is.

▷ A microscope makes things look much bigger than a magnifying glass does. It has lots of lenses inside, and can make things look hundreds of times bigger than they really are. This scientist is using a microscope to examine some of the tiny living things that cause disease.

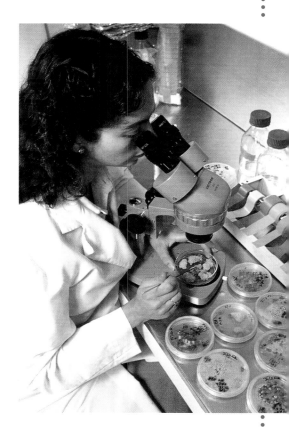

◁ With some people, the rays of light passing into their eyes do not bend enough to make a clear picture. With others, the rays may bend too much. The lenses in spectacles help people to see more clearly by correcting the amount the rays are bent.

Find out more
Day and Night
Energy
Mirrors
Senses
Television

Lion

Lions are the largest predators in Africa. These powerful big cats live in groups called prides in bush country or on grassy plains. A pride is made up of several females and their cubs, as well as a few males. Apart from humans, the lion has no enemies and is known as the 'king of the beasts'.

▽ Lions hunt mainly at night and spend the day resting. They prey on many of the large animals of the plains, including antelope, zebra and buffalo. As well as looking after the cubs, the lionesses (female lions) do most of the hunting.

△ The male lion has a large, shaggy mane around its neck. It is his job to defend the territory of his pride and he will warn off intruders with a loud roar. Adult lions have tawny coats, but lion cubs have spots.

Find out more
Cheetah
Mammal
Tiger

Living things

A living thing grows, feeds, breathes and can reproduce (make young). The two main types of living things are plants and animals. Animals are living things that can move about. They eat other living things as food. Plants are living things that stay in one place. They make their own food using the energy from sunlight.

parrots

Vertebrates
All the animals on this side of the page are vertebrates. This means each one has a skeleton and a backbone inside its body.

butterfly

snake

chimpanzee

amoeba

scorpion

Invertebrates
All the animals on this side of the page are invertebrates. They do not have backbones or skeletons. Some have hard cases or shells to protect their soft bodies. Some invertebrates, such as the amoeba, are tiny one-celled creatures.

worm

frog

sting ray

spider

starfish

snail

169

▽ Plants use energy from sunlight, and water and minerals from the soil to make their own food. Many plants make flowers seeds. The seeds grow into new plants.

flower

stem

leaf

root

△ Some animals, such as this bear, hibernate in winter. This means they go into a kind of deep sleep. This saves energy, as they do not need to go out and hunt for food.

▽ Sea anemones look like plants but are really animals. They use their tentacles to catch small creatures to eat.

▽ There are hundreds of thousands of different kinds of plants. Some are so tiny that you can only see them through a microscope. Others, such as trees, can be huge.

△ Animals must find food to eat, or they will die. Some animals eat plants. Others, like this fish eagle, eat animals. Some animals, such as humans, eat both plants and animals.

Habitats

Arctic

desert

rainforest

grassy plain

▽ Dodos were a kind of bird that lived on a small island in the Indian Ocean. People killed so many for food that now there are no dodos left at all. They are extinct.

◁ Rhinoceroses are in danger of becoming extinct (dying out). One reason for this is because so many have been killed by hunters for their precious horns. This rhinoceros's horns have been cut off, to protect it.

◁ The places where plants and animals live are called their habitats. Animals and plants are usually specially suited to their particular habitats. Arctic animals have thick coats to keep them warm in the icy cold. Desert plants and animals need very little water to stay alive.

◁ Rainforests are home to about half of all the types of plants and animals in the world. In the grassy plains of Africa, hunters, such as lions, lie in wait to prey on antelopes and zebras.

Find out more
Air and
Atmosphere
Day and Night
Earth
Human body
Medicine
Senses
Water

Lizard

Lizards are reptiles. They have scaly skin, long tails and usually live in warm countries. Although they can dart about very quickly, they are cold blooded and need to lie in the sun to keep warm.

△ The Gila monster is a lizard that lives in the North American deserts. Bright red and black markings warn that it has a poisonous bite.

△ Many lizards turn darker when basking in the sun. This helps their bodies to absorb its heat better.

△ The Australian thorny devil looks frightening, but it is harmless. Its sharp spines save it from being eaten by predators.

Fact box

• The smallest lizards, the geckos of the Virgin Islands, are 35 millimetres long.
• If some species of lizard are caught by the tail, the tail breaks off. A new one will grow in its place within eight months.

◁ The frilled lizard of Australia lifts up its huge neck collar to scare off attackers.

Find out more
Chameleon

Llama

The llama is found in the high Andes mountains and on the dry plains of South America. Like its relative, the alpaca, it is tame. They are both relatives of the wild guanaco. All three are members of the camel family.

△ Guanacos usually live on mountains over 4,000 metres high, although they are also found on the lower plains. Their blood is rich in red cells, which helps them to breathe the thin mountain air.

△ Today, llamas are used mainly as pack animals, as they were by the ancient Inca people of Peru. Female llamas are used for meat, but males are too tough to eat.

▷ Alpaca wool is prized by the local South American people. It has a soft feel and provides warmth in the cold climate.

Find out more
Camel
Goat
Mammal
Yak

Machines

Machines are things that make jobs easier and quicker to do. Some machines are very simple. For example, a hammer is a simple machine – so is a wheelbarrow, and so is a pair of scissors. People have used simple machines like these for thousands of years.

▽ **1** Make and use a simple machine. Start by putting some heavy books on a table. Try lifting them with your finger. It's hard work. Next, slide one end of a ruler under the books.

1

▷ **2** Lift up the end of the ruler. This makes the books much easier to move. The ruler is working as a machine called a lever. We often use levers to help us lift things.

2

△ A slope does not look much like a machine. But it can be used as one because it makes getting to a high point easier than climbing straight upwards.

pliers

wheelbarrow

▽ Many of the machines we use at home need electricity to make them work.

hairdryer

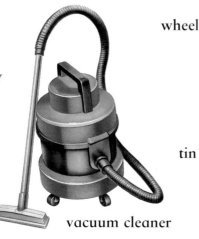

vacuum cleaner

tin opener

◁ Pliers, a wheelbarrow and a tin opener are all examples of levers. When you push or pull one part of a lever, such as the pliers' handles, you make a push or pull on another part, such as the pliers' tips.

△ A combine harvester is a complicated machine made of several machines rolled into one. It cuts the corn and threshes it, to get the grain from the straw (stems). Then it packs the straw into bales.

◁ A pulley is a machine that helps you to lift heavy objects. It is made of a rope that runs around one or more wheels. As you pull down on one end of the rope, the other end rises and lifts whatever is attached to it.

▷ Cars, aircraft and trains are all transport machines that move people and goods from place to place. They all have engines that turn fuel into energy, to turn their wheels or make them fly.

◁ A bicycle is made up of many simple machines that work together. For example, the pedals and gears are simple machines that make pedalling easier. The brakes are simple machines to help slow the wheels down.

Find out more
Energy
Engines
Force
Technology

175

Magnets

Have you ever tried to pick up a piece of paper with a magnet? It can't be done! Magnets can only pick up things made from certain kinds of metals. The most common of these are iron and steel. The force or pull that magnets exert is called magnetic force.

△ The area around a magnet is called its magnetic field. This is as far as its power stretches. To see a magnetic field, put a magnet on a sheet of paper and sprinkle some iron filings around it. The filings cluster inside the magnetic field, around the magnet's poles (ends).

fridge magnet

▽ One end of the magnet is called its north pole and the other is its south pole. Two north poles facing each other push each other apart. So do two south poles facing each other. But if a north pole faces a south pole, they pull towards each other.

△ The Earth has its own magnetic field. It is as if the Earth has a huge bar-shaped magnet running through it, with its poles near the Earth's North and South poles.

the Earth's magnetic field

fridge magnet

◁ The needle in a compass is actually a magnet. It swings around until its north pole points north – towards the Earth's magnetic north pole.

▽ This train travels by floating along, just above a rail. There is a magnet inside the train and the rail is a magnet, too. The two magnets are arranged so that they push each other away. Because of this, the train floats above the rail as it moves.

◁ Make some fishes from foil. Fix a paperclip to each one. Make two toy fishing rods by tying magnets to pieces of string. Have a competition with a friend. Dangle the rods above the fishes. Who catches the most?

1

◁ **1** You can make a magnet using electricity. This kind of magnet is called an electromagnet. You need some thin plastic-covered wire, a steel nail and a torch battery. Start by winding the wire around the nail. Wind all the way up and down the nail until the wire is about three layers thick.

fridge magnet

2

▷ **2** Fix one end of the wire to the top of a torch battery and the other end to the bottom, so that you have made a circuit. Now try picking up a paperclip or a steel drawing pin with the nail. What happens when you disconnect the battery?

Find out more
Battery
Earth
Electricity
Force
Machines
Materials
Recording
Television

Mammals

Mammals are animals whose young are fed with their mother's milk. Most mammals give birth to live young.

The biggest mammal is the blue whale, which can be as long as six elephants. One of the smallest is a kind of bat that is about the size of a bumble bee.

rabbit

△ A rabbit gives birth to lots of babies at the same time. A mother rabbit cares for her young until they can look after themselves.

◁ Humans are mammals too. When we are babies we are fed with our mother's milk.

humans

▷ A kangaroo is a marsupial, a mammal that carries its young in a pouch. A baby kangaroo is called a joey.

kangaroo

lion

▷ Lions live in family groups called prides. They eat meat and are fierce hunters. A lioness cares for her cubs and teaches them how to hunt.

mole

▽ A mole is a burrowing mammal. It has strong front legs and big claws for digging holes called burrows.

cubs

dolphins

◁ Dolphins are mammals that live in the sea. They have to come to the surface to breathe.

bat

△ Bats are the only mammals that can fly. A bat has a furry body and its wings are soft, smooth skin.

chimpanzees

Fact box

• Most mammals have either hair or fur.

• Mammals are warm-blooded. This means that the temperature of their bodies stays the same in both hot and cold weather.

• A mammal is a vertebrate, which means that it has a backbone.

• Mammals have larger brains than other animals.

▽ The duck-billed platypus is an unusual mammal because it lays eggs.

duck-billed platypus

△ Chimpanzees live in family groups. They often comb each other's hair with their fingers and pick off dirt and ticks.

Etruscan shrew

lioness

△ The tiny Etruscan shrew weighs no more than a sugar lump.

Find out more
Animals
Australia and the Pacific Islands
Babies
Caves
Grasslands
Human body
Prehistoric life

179

Materials

Look around your classroom. Can you see clothes, shoes, chairs, tables and books? What are these things made of? Some are made of plastic, and others are made of metal, wood or fabrics. These are all materials. Different materials have different uses. For example, shoes are often made from leather or plastic because these are strong and will bend.

▷ These things are made from clay. Clay is a kind of soft earth that can be formed into different shapes. When it is baked it becomes very hard. Things made from clay are called ceramics.

Fact box
- Paper was invented in China about 2,000 years ago.
- Weaving is done on a machine called a loom. The first looms were made about 8,000 years ago.
- Before people found out about metals, they made tools, such as axes, from flint stone.

Make a kite

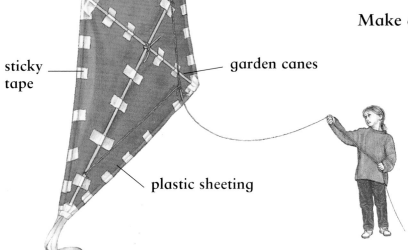

sticky tape

garden canes

plastic sheeting

ribbons

◁ What sort of materials would you use to make a kite like this one? Remember, a kite must be made of something light, so it will fly. It must be strong, so that it does not tear in the wind.

△ This kite's frame is made from thin garden canes. It is covered with plastic sheeting. The flying line is light, strong fishing line.

◁ Everything in this picture is made from plastic. Plastics are synthetic materials, which means they are made in factories, from chemicals.

Some kinds of plastics are hard and stiff. Others are soft and bendy.

△ Re-using materials instead of throwing them away is called recycling. For example, these bottles are going to be recycled. They may be used again, or the glass may be melted down to make new bottles.

▷ Fabric is a word for cloth. Fabrics are made by weaving or knitting fibres (thin strands) together. Wool and cotton are called natural fibres because they come from animals or plants. Synthetic fibres, such as nylon, are made from chemicals.

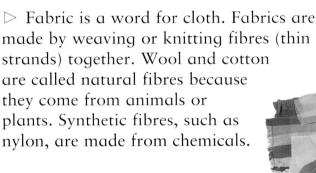

◁ Most metals are hard and shiny. They can be made into different shapes and sharpened, to make knives and tools. Many metals are very strong and can get very hot before they melt. This means they are a good material for saucepans.

◁ In many parts of the world, the materials people use in their everyday lives are the ones they can find nearby. For example, these boats are made from reeds that grow on the lake where their owners live.

Find out more
Fuels
Technology

181

Mathematics

Mathematics is the study of numbers and how we use them. Most people use some mathematics every day, to count their money, add up their shopping, measure things or keep the score in games. Many people use mathematics in their work.

For example, scientists and engineers use mathematics to make calculations and keep records of their results.

△ Do you do sums like these at school? Adding, subtracting, multiplying and dividing numbers is called arithmetic. Arithmetic is just one part of mathematics.

▷ Mathematicians sometimes use charts and graphs to show information in ways that are easier to understand than long lists of numbers.

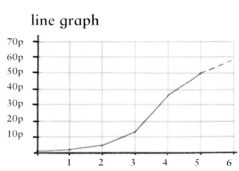

line graph

△ This line graph shows how someone's pocket money went up over six years.

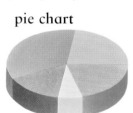

pie chart

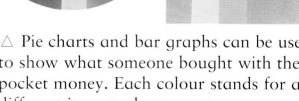

bar graph

△ Pie charts and bar graphs can be used to show what someone bought with their pocket money. Each colour stands for a different item, such as sweets or toys.

◁ Geometry is the part of mathematics that is about studying shapes. These girls are arranging hexagons to see how these shapes fit together neatly without leaving any gaps.

Find out more
Calculator
Experiment
Numbers

Measurement

How can you tell how long, how tall, how heavy, how hot or how cold something is? The answer is by measuring it.

Measurements are made in units. For example, we use grams and kilograms for weight, metres and kilometres for length and degrees for temperature.

△ In some countries, people measure long distances in kilometres. In others, they use miles. These road signs in Australia and the United States show both. Eight kilometres is equal to five miles.

◁ This girl is measuring the length of the boy's arm. She is using a tape measure. Tape measures show units of length. Some show centimetres and metres. Others show inches and feet. Some show both, so you can choose which units you use.

△ The amount of space something takes up is called its volume. This jug is for measuring the volume of liquids. The units used are litres or pints.

▷ Try some measuring. Use a stop watch to measure how long it takes different children to walk or run the same distance. Ask a friend to write down the times. Who is the fastest?

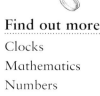

Find out more
Clocks
Mathematics
Numbers

Medicine

Medicine is the study of health, illnesses and injuries. When someone is ill, they might ask a doctor for help. The doctor uses a knowledge of medicine to find out what is wrong, and help the patient get better. Many illnesses can be cured with chemicals, called drugs. These are also sometimes called medicines.

▽ Sometimes, a sick person needs an operation. A doctor called a surgeon makes a cut to reach inside the body. A drug called an anaesthetic is used to stop the person feeling any pain.

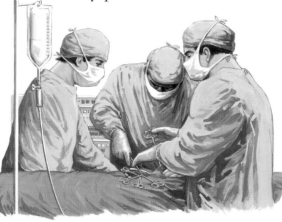

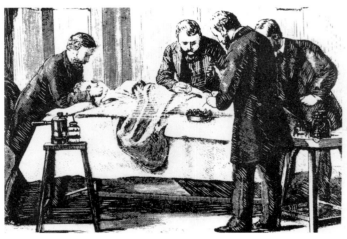

◁ This picture shows the first time doctors used antiseptics. These are chemicals that kill germs. Antiseptics were first used in operations in 1867. Before this, people often died after operations from infections caused by germs.

acanthus

chicory

△ For thousands of years, people have used special plants to treat illnesses. Many modern drugs also contain chemicals found in plants.

Never touch or swallow any medicines or plants unless they are given to you by an adult.

△ Sometimes doctors give us injections containing a special kind of drug, called a vaccine. Vaccines help to stop us from catching diseases, such as measles.

Find out more
Biology
Chemistry and Chemicals
Technology
X-rays

Meerkat

Meerkats are small meat-eating mammals. The word meerkat means 'marsh cat'. However, they actually live on the dry, open plains of Africa, not on marshes. They are known for their comic way of standing on their hind legs, on the lookout for predators.

△ Meerkats live in burrows under the ground. They come out during the day to hunt for food, but they are always watching out for eagles and other birds of prey.

▽ Meerkats often hunt by digging for prey with their long, sharp claws. They also look for insects, eggs, small animals and plant roots to eat. They have a good sense of smell, and can see and hear well.

△ Like the meerkat, the mongoose will often attack poisonous snakes, in order to defend its burrow and its young.

Find out more
Cat (wild)
Cobra
Mammal

Melting and Boiling

Melting is when a solid turns into a liquid. Boiling turns liquid into a gas. These are called changes of state because they change a substance from one state of matter to another. A substance needs heat to make it melt or boil. There are two other changes of state. When gases cool, they may condense and become liquid. Liquids can be turned into solids by cooling or freezing.

△ What happens if you don't eat your ice lolly quickly enough? It melts in the warm air. The solid ice turns to liquid.

 Take care! Never touch or move anything with hot or boiling liquid in it. You could get badly burned.

△ This flask is full of nitrogen. Nitrogen is normally a gas, but if it is made very cold it condenses and turns into a liquid. In this picture, you can see it turning back into a gas in the warm air.

△ When you heat water, it gets hotter and hotter until the temperature reaches 100°C (212°F). It then boils and starts to turn into a gas called water vapour.

◁ Watch how a gas turns into liquid when it is cooled. Breathe onto a mirror. Water vapour in your breath cools when it reaches the surface of the mirror and turns into liquid (water).

Find out more
Energy
Gases
Solids

Metals

Metals are quite often hard, shiny materials. They can be bent or hammered into different shapes. Iron, copper and aluminium are three kinds of metal. Most metals come from ores, which are a mixture of metal and rock. The ore is dug out of the ground. Different metals can be mixed to make tough, new metals, called alloys.

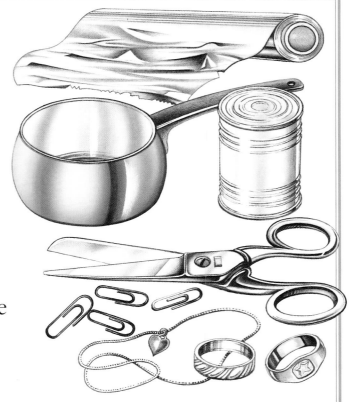

△ Aluminium is used to make foil, cans and pipes, copper is used for saucepans, steel for scissors and paperclips, and gold and silver are used to make jewellery.

△ Iron ore is heated in a furnace. When it gets very hot, the iron melts. The iron is then poured off, leaving the unwanted rock behind. The iron is then used to make steel.

▽ Iron turns rusty if it is left in damp air. Rusty metal is weak and crumbles away. Often metal things are specially treated to stop them rusting.

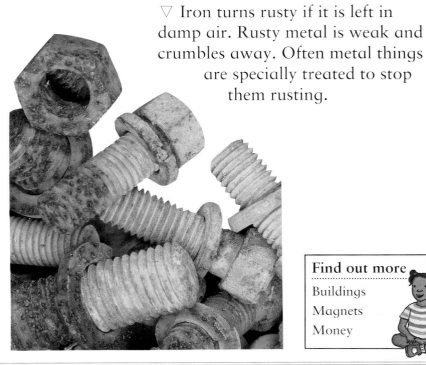

Find out more
Buildings
Magnets
Money

Microscopic animal

Some animals are so tiny that they can only be seen through a microscope. They live almost everywhere – in the water, in the air, in the ground and even in your bed.

△ A good way to see microscopic animals is to look at pondwater through a microscope. Take a note of what you see as you look at the slide. You will probably see animals called daphnia, also known as water fleas.

△ Amoebas are among the tiniest living things. They move by changing shape.

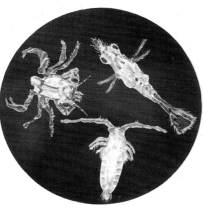

▷ Zooplankton are tiny creatures that drift in water. They are the food of the world's biggest animal, the blue whale.

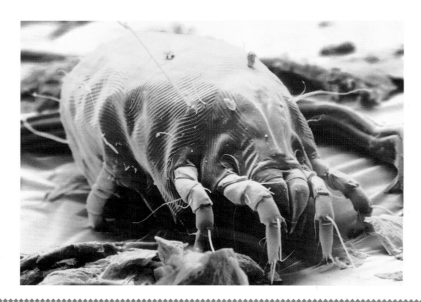

◁ House-dust mites are invisible to the naked eye. They feed on flakes of skin that they find in bedding and soft fabrics. These eight-legged creatures are related to spiders and there are millions of them in the average home.

Find out more
Beetle
Reproduction
Spider

Microwaves

Do you have a microwave oven in your kitchen? Microwaves are used in cooking, but they can also carry messages and signals through air and space. Satellite television programmes are carried by microwaves. When you make an international telephone call, microwaves may carry the call up to a communications satellite in space, and then back down to Earth.

△ The dishes at the top of this tower send and pick up microwaves. These carry long-distance telephone calls.

Never put anything in a microwave oven without asking an adult first.

▽ This is a microwave oven. Microwaves are beamed into the food. They make the atoms in the food jiggle about. When this happens, the food gets hot and cooks.

◁ A fan scatters the microwaves about so that they reach every part of the food being cooked.

▷ There is a machine inside the oven that makes the microwaves.

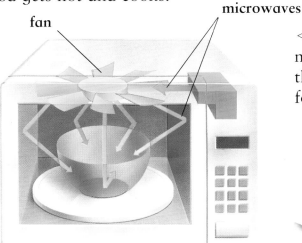

fan

microwaves

▷ Ships and aircraft use radar to detect objects around them. A radar dish sends out beams of microwaves. If these strike an object, they bounce back to the dish and the object shows up on a screen linked to the dish.

Find out more
Light and Lenses
Radio
X-rays

Migration

Many animals make journeys from one place to another to find better living conditions. Some move quite short distances, but others travel from one side of the world to the other. These regular return trips are known as migration.

▷ In autumn, you may see 'V' formations of Canada geese flying overhead. Make a note of when they leave and in which direction they go. Watch for their return in spring.

▽ The Earth is criss-crossed with animal migration routes. Use the colour-keyed arrows on the map to see where these four migrating species travel each year.

■ Canada geese (above) fly to the Arctic Circle in the spring to breed. In autumn, they return to warmer southern regions.

■ Grey whales spend the winter in the warm sea off California, where they give birth to their calves. In summer, they swim north to the rich food supplies in Alaskan waters.

■ Arctic terns travel further than any other animal. Each year, they move from pole to pole and back again.

■ Swifts spend the summer in Europe, where they catch insects to feed their young. They spend the winter in Africa.

◁ Many grass-eating animals in Africa migrate to find food. Like these wildebeest, they follow the rain as it moves.

Find out more
Arctic tern
Reindeer

Mirrors

A mirror is a smooth, shiny surface that reflects nearly all the light that hits it. You can see yourself in a mirror because light reflects from you to the mirror and then bounces off the mirror and back into your eyes. Most mirrors are made of glass. Mirrors are not simply for looking at yourself. They have many other uses, too.

△ The back of a mirror is painted silver. Light bounces off this smooth layer of silver paint and into your eyes.

◁ How many other shiny surfaces can you find? Metals are very shiny. Other very smooth things, such as china plates, are shiny, too.

▷ Astronomers use large, powerful telescopes to look at the stars. These have mirrors inside them. The mirrors are curved like shallow dishes. They work in the same sort of way as lenses, to make things look nearer.

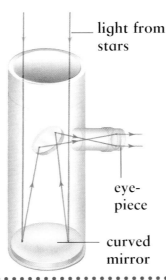

light from stars

eye-piece

curved mirror

△ Look at your reflection in a mirror. The mirror reflects your image straight out again so everything looks back to front. See if you can work out how this happens.

Find out more
Light and Lenses

Mole

Moles are small mammals that spend almost all their lives underground. We know they are around because of the molehills they create when digging their tunnels. They live in Europe, Asia and North America.

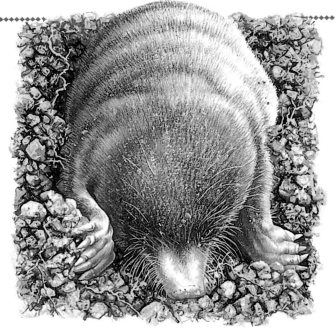

△ Big, powerful front paws, a pointed nose and sharp claws mean that moles are excellent diggers. Although they have bad eyesight, they hunt for worms and insects using their good sense of smell and by picking up vibrations with their whiskers.

△ Baby moles are born in a nest, called a fortress, deep below a molehill. They are lucky to be born at all – like all moles, their parents fought furiously when they first met.

◁ When moles dig tunnels they push the earth to the surface, which makes molehills. These are more common in autumn, when young moles look for new areas to live.

Fact box
- Moles surface at night to search for nest material.
- The star-nosed mole has a star of sensitive fleshy tentacles on its nose.
- People used to make clothes from mole fur.

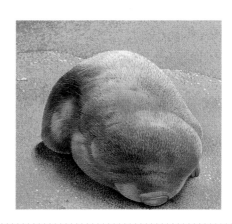

◁ Golden moles are found in dry places in Africa. They live underground and burrow through sand to find food. Like all moles, they have very soft and silky coats.

Find out more
Badger
Mammal
Mouse

Money

Money is used to pay for the things we want to buy. Coins and paper notes are money. Each coin and note is worth a different amount. People use notes for large amounts. Notes are printed with complicated patterns that are hard to fake, or copy.

△ Before money existed, people swapped the things they needed. This is called barter. The man on the left is bartering his cattle for armour.

▷ You can save your coins in a money box. Large amounts of money are kept in a bank.

◁ Each country has its own type of money. Great Britain uses pounds, America uses dollars and France uses francs.

Find out more

Jobs

Metal

Monkey

Monkeys are clever mammals that can solve problems and hold things in their hands. They live in groups called troops, high in the tropical forests of the Americas, Africa and Asia. Monkeys eat plants, birds' eggs, small animals and insects.

△ A monkey's eyes face forwards, which helps it to see well when hunting. Most monkeys hunt by day.

△ Howler monkeys come from South America and are good climbers. They use their tails as an extra 'hand' when swinging through the branches. Howler monkeys live in groups headed by an old male. They get their name from the loud calls the group makes together to warn other monkeys off their territory.

▷ The capuchin monkey is a small monkey that lives in the Amazon jungle. Because of its intelligence and curious nature, many have been kept as pets and taught to do tricks.

▽ The proboscis monkey of Borneo gets its name from its big nose. It has a long tail too, but uses it only for balance.

Fact box
• One difference between monkeys and apes is that monkeys have tails, while apes do not.
• A female monkey usually has one baby or, sometimes, twins.

Find out more
Baboon
Chimpanzee
Gorilla
Orang-utann

Moon

The Moon is our nearest neighbour in Space. It is a large ball of dusty rock with no air, water, wind or weather. No animals or plants can live there. During the day it is boiling hot, but at night it is very cold. The Moon looks bright in the sky because it reflects light from the Sun.

▽ The Moon moves around the Earth once every month. Its path is called an orbit.

△ The Moon is covered with dents called craters. These were made when meteoroids crashed into the Moon. Meteoroids are large lumps of rock and metal.

Full Moon

△ There is a Full Moon once a month. As the Sun lights up different parts of the Moon, its shape seems to change.

▽ On 20th July 1969, two American astronauts were the first people to set foot on the Moon. They were called Neil Armstrong and Buzz Aldrin.

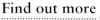

Find out more

Planets

Space exploration

Motion

Motion is another word for movement. Things cannot start to move on their own. They need a force (a push or a pull) to get them started. Once something has started to move, a force can make it move faster, or it can slow it down again. Speeding up motion is called acceleration. Slowing it down is called deceleration.

△ This shot-putter uses force to get the shot moving through the air. Gravity pulls at the shot as it travels along. It slows the shot down and then pulls it back to the ground.

◁ 1 A moving object will always try to keep moving, and a still object will try to stay still. This is called inertia. Try this experiment. Put a raw egg on a tray and spin it. As the egg spins, the runny yolk inside it spins, too.

▷ 2 Stop the egg, then quickly let go of it. It starts to spin again. This is because the yoke inside the egg has inertia. It goes on moving when you stop the shell. When you let go of the shell, inertia starts the egg moving again.

Fact box
• People used to try to make machines called perpetual motion machines, that would keep on moving for ever. None of these machines ever worked, as friction always made them stop.

△ The faster a car is going, the longer it takes for it to stop. That is why it is important for drivers to go slowly in places where people may be crossing the road.

▷ Moving objects always try to keep going in a straight line. The boy is swinging the weight on the end of this string in a circle. The weight needs a force to keep it moving in a circle. The force comes from the string. Without it, the weight would fly off in a straight line.

△ These heavy railway wagons need a lot of force to make them move. The locomotives had to exert a huge pull on them to get them started. Heavy things are harder to get moving and harder to slow down than light things.

▽ A grasshopper is light and small. Its legs give a huge push compared to its size, which helps it to accelerate very fast when it hops away.

Find out more
Energy
Flight
Force

Mountains

A mountain is a piece of ground that is much higher than the land around it. The highest peaks are cold and windy. They are often covered with snow all year. Tough pine trees grow on the lower slopes. Above a certain height, it is too cold for trees to grow.

◁ Skiing is a fast way to get across snow. It is a popular mountain sport.

rocky mountain goat

△ Mountain goats have thick, woolly coats and are good climbers.

trumpet gentian

△ The cold winds mean that mountain plants can only grow in low clumps.

Find out more
Asia
Europe
Oceans and seas
South America
Volcano

Mouse

Mice are small rodents with long tails and sharp front teeth. These grow all the time, so mice must gnaw things to stop them from getting too long. There are many kinds of wild mouse, found all over the world. Mice can also be kept as pets.

△ Mice eat many foods, including seeds, grain, roots, fruit and insects. They also enjoy human food. The house mouse lives in people's homes.

△ American harvest mice are good at climbing. They build globe-shaped nests above the ground on the stems of grasses.

▽ Test how clever your pet mouse is with this mouse-maze. Cut some cardboard into strips 15 centimetres wide, then glue the strips to a wooden board in a maze pattern. Put some food at the end of the maze and see how long your mouse takes to find it. Repeat to see if it gets quicker at solving the maze.

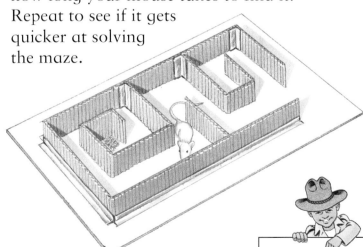

◁ Dormice live in Europe, Africa and Asia. Unlike many other mice, they have furry tails. Dormice make nests from plants and, in cold places, sleep through winter.

Find out more
Beaver
Food
Guinea pig, Gerbil and Hamster
Rat

Music

Most people love to play or listen to music. They may sing or play a musical instrument, like a piano or a guitar, by themselves or in a band or orchestra. People play music to celebrate special occasions, to entertain themselves or others, or just to relax. A person who makes music is called a musician. There are many different kinds of music.

△ You probably listen to music on tapes, CDs and records at home, or hear it on the radio and television.

△ An orchestra is a large group of musicians who play a variety of different instruments. Orchestras often play the music at concerts, operas or plays.

▷ At carnival time in the Caribbean islands, steel bands play in the streets or on the beach. The steel drums are made out of specially shaped, empty oil drums.

▷ This Japanese robot can play the keyboard much faster than a human can. It can read music or play a tune that is stored in its memory.

WABOT - 2

▽ You can play music too. You may know how to play the piano or the recorder. There are many other kinds of musical instruments. These children are making music with their instruments.

triangle

cymbal

tambourine

◁ One of the most famous musicians was Wolfgang Amadeus Mozart. It's hard to believe that he wrote his first piece of music when he was only five years old.

Find out more
Australia
Dance
Sound

North America

North America is the third largest continent. In the north it is cold and there are large forests and many lakes. In the south there are hot deserts and thick rainforests. The middle is a huge area of flat grassland, called the prairie. The magnificent Rocky Mountains run down one side. Many of its people live in busy, modern cities.

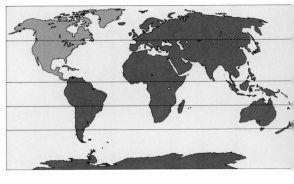

△ North America is shown in blue on this map. Most of it is covered by two very large countries, Canada and the United States of America.

◁ Many people visit Las Vegas in the USA. It was built in the middle of the desert. At night its buildings are lit up with their bright lights.

△ A teacher and her class at a school in the United States. People of many different nationalities have come to live and work in America.

◁ A stall owner getting ready for market day in Oaxaca, in Mexico. Mexican farmers were the first people to grow chillies, tomatoes, avocados, maize and many kinds of beans.

△ Thanksgiving Day is a national holiday in America. Families gather together to eat a traditional meal of roast turkey and pumpkin pie.

▽ The Grand Canyon in Arizona is one of the most famous sights in the United States. It was carved by a river flowing through the desert.

◁ Raccoons live in many parts of North America. They usually hunt at night for food.

raccoon

▷ The Niagara Falls lie on the border between Canada and the United States. Tourists take boats to see the base of the falls.

◁ The word pueblo is Spanish for village. Pueblo are Native American people who live in south-western USA.

Find out more

Buildings
Desert
Grasslands
History
Sports
World
Year

Nuclear energy

Everything that exists is made up of atoms. An atom is made up of a nucleus, surrounded by electrons. If a nucleus breaks apart, a huge amount of energy is released. This is called nuclear energy. In a nuclear power station, this is used to make electricity. When atoms break apart, they also give out rays called radioactivity. Things that give off radioactivity are called radioactive.

△ Massive amounts of energy are formed in the Sun. There, atoms join together instead of splitting apart. This is another way that nuclear energy is created.

◁ Inside a nuclear power station, nuclear reactors split atoms apart and release energy as heat. This heat is used to produce electrical energy.

▷ This sign means "Danger! Radioactivity!" It is used wherever there are radioactive substances. These can be very dangerous, causing burns and diseases in people and animals.

▷ An atom bomb makes a massive explosion. Billions of atoms split up at the same time and an enormous amount of energy is released. After the explosion, dangerous nuclear radiation is left behind for many years.

Find out more
Energy
Fuels
Solar System
Universe

Numbers

We use numbers in many different ways. We use them for counting, for writing down measurements and for doing sums. We also use them for labelling things, such as the houses in a street and telephone numbers.

Numbers are shown as symbols, called digits. For example, the number 368 has three digits – 3, 6 and 8.

▽ We count and do sums using numbers in groups. For example, in 235, the 2 means two hundreds, the 3 means three tens and the 5 means five ones. This system of numbers is called base ten.

△ The numbers we use today were invented in India over 1,000 years ago. Arab traders started using them and brought them to Europe.

2 hundreds

3 tens

5 ones

△ Around the world people write numbers differently. They were also different in the past. Medieval numbers were used in Europe in the 12th and 13th centuries. Roman numbers are still used today.

Fact box

• Before numbers were invented, people carved a notch on a stick or bone to keep count of things. Sometimes, they made a pile of stones instead. Counting this way is called keeping a tally.

▷ Computers do calculations using a system of numbers called the binary system. They use only two digits – 0 and 1. Here you can see how to write the numbers 0 to 8 in the binary system.

binary numbers

Find out more

Calculator
Clocks
Computers
Mathematics
Measurement

Oceans and seas

There are four huge areas of water called oceans – the Pacific, the Atlantic, the Indian and the Arctic. The Pacific is by far the biggest and deepest ocean. Seas are smaller areas of water. There is more water than land on the Earth's surface. You can sail right around the world without touching land.

△ Most waves are made by wind blowing across the water. Surfers ride on them before they crash on to the shore. Some waves are ten metres tall.

◁ There are strange animals in the deepest, darkest parts of the ocean. Some have large mouths and glowing lights to help them catch their prey.

▽ At the bottom of the ocean there are flat areas, trenches, hills and high mountains. Some islands are the tops of underwater volcanoes.

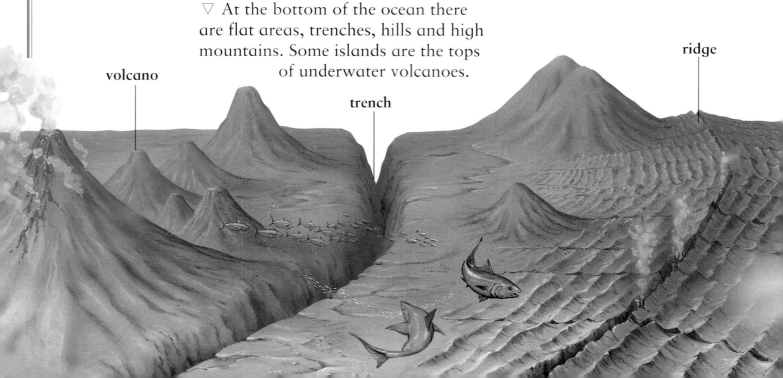

volcano

trench

ridge

▷ There are billions of tiny plants and animals floating in the sea. They are called plankton. Many fish and other sea creatures feed on them.

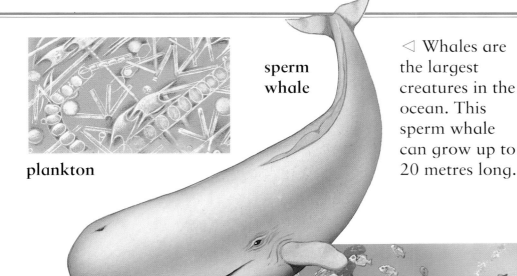

plankton

sperm whale

◁ Whales are the largest creatures in the ocean. This sperm whale can grow up to 20 metres long.

▽ An octopus has eight long arms. If an octopus loses an arm, it grows a new one.

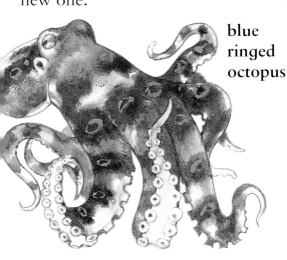

blue ringed octopus

▷ For hundreds of years ships have sunk to the bottom of the sea. Divers sometimes find treasure in the remains of these ships.

▽ Divers use small submersibles to explore very deep water. They dive down to search for shipwrecks and to study ocean life.

submersible

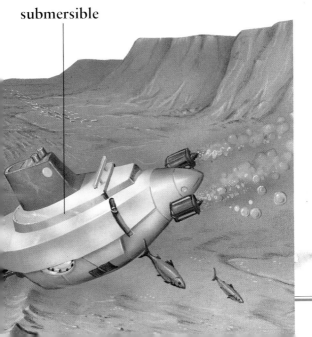

▽ Hot water bubbles up through chimney-like holes on the sea bed. Blind crabs, giant worms and other unusual creatures live near these rare hot spots.

worms

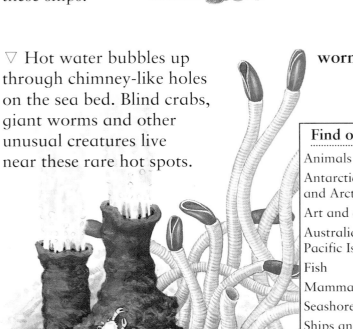

crabs

Find out more

Animals

Antarctica and Arctic

Art and artists

Australia and the Pacific Islands

Fish

Mammals

Seashore

Ships and boats

Water

World

Octopus and Squid

The octopus is a sea creature with eight long arms, called tentacles. These can wind round objects and have suckers on them that grip. The squid is related to the octopus, but it has ten arms.

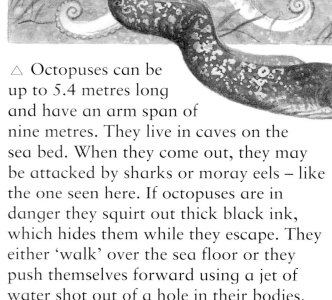

◁ Squid range in length from 1.5 centimetres right up to 20 metres for the largest species. Two of their ten arms are especially long and have suckers on the end.

△ Octopuses can be up to 5.4 metres long and have an arm span of nine metres. They live in caves on the sea bed. When they come out, they may be attacked by sharks or moray eels – like the one seen here. If octopuses are in danger they squirt out thick black ink, which hides them while they escape. They either 'walk' over the sea floor or they push themselves forward using a jet of water shot out of a hole in their bodies.

◁ Octopuses ambush their prey, such as crabs, shellfish and shrimps. Their tentacles draw the victim towards their powerful, birdlike beak. This is hidden at the base of the tentacles.

Find out more
Crab
Shellfish
Starfish

Orang-utan

The word orang-utan means 'man of the forest' in the Malay language, and it is true that this large ape does look a bit like an old, hairy man. Orang-utans live in Southeast Asia.

▷ Baby orang-utans are reared by their mothers and will stay with them until they are around five years old.

△ Orang-utans have become rare partly because their forest habitat has been cut down, but also because some people think baby orang-utans make good pets, and steal them from the wild. Mothers are often killed while defending their babies.

▽ Orang-utans have long, strong arms. They climb slowly through the trees in the morning and evening searching for wild figs – their favourite food. At night they sleep on platforms made of branches.

Find out more
Baboon
Chimpanzee
Gorilla
Monkey

Ostrich, Emu and Cassowary

Not all birds can fly. Although they have small wings, the world's biggest birds – ostriches, cassowaries and emus – can only walk and run.

▽ Emus are the second tallest birds, growing to 1.8 metres. They live on the grasslands of Australia.

△ Ostriches lay up to eight giant eggs in a nest on the ground. The male sits on the eggs at night; the female, during the day.

▽ Male ostriches are black and white. They are the biggest birds of all – often 2.5 metres tall. Females are slightly smaller and greyish-brown. They can run at 65 kilometres per hour.

Fact box

• Ostriches live in Africa.
• Ostrich eggs are the biggest of all bird eggs.

◁ Cassowaries live in the forests of New Guinea and Australia. They are 1.5 metres tall and have featherless heads with a bony helmet on the top. If attacked, they will kick and slash with their clawed feet. Their middle toe is as sharp as a dagger.

Find out more
Bird

Otter

Otters are mammals found near rivers and seashores around the world. Although the otter makes its home on the land, it spends much of its time in the water.

△ Female otters give birth to between one and five young in an underground burrow called a holt.

long tail: this acts like as ship's rudder to steer the otter

fur: two layers keep the otter warm and dry

eyes and nose: on top of the head so the otter can see and breathe while swimming

whiskers: help the otter feel movements in the water

teeth: long, sharp teeth grip and bite prey and crack shells

▷ Otters eat fish and small animals. They are strong swimmers and well designed for hunting in the water.

feet: webbed feet for swimming fast

claws: sharp claws help the otter to dig

▽ Young otters spend lots of time playing and wrestling with each other. One of their favourite games is to slide down a snow or mud bank.

△ Sea otters are found along the northern rim of the Pacific Ocean – from California to northern Japan. They often float on their backs and sometimes carry their young on their bellies.

Find out more
Beaver
Platypus
Seal and Sea lion

Owl

Owls are birds of prey that hunt mainly at night. They use their sensitive hearing and large eyes (which give them good night vision) to catch animals such as mice and rabbits. Owls have soft feathers that allow them to fly silently. The hooting cry of some species is easy to recognize.

△ Tawny owls were once found only in woodlands. Today, they also live in towns and cities, where they hunt mice and rats. During the day, they settle in the trees of parks and gardens.

◁ The burrowing owls of North and South America live in burrows in the ground. They either dig a hole themselves or use one left by another animal, such as a gopher.

▽ Barn owls build nests in buildings, hollow trees or old hawk's nests. The round, flat shape of the barn owl's head helps it to hear its prey. Once it has caught the animal, the adult brings it to the chicks in the nest.

Fact box

- Owls can swivel their heads almost all the way round when they are listening for sounds.
- Snowy owls live in the Arctic. They mainly hunt lemmings. These owls nest on the ground.

Find out more

Bat
Bird
Eagle

Panda

The giant panda is a bear found in just a few high bamboo forests in China. There are probably no more than 1,500 giant pandas left in the wild. About 100 are kept in zoos around the world.

▽ Pandas have one or two cubs at a time. At birth, a cub weighs only 100 grams. At first the mother holds it close to her chest at all times. But it grows quickly and after ten weeks the cub starts to crawl.

△ Giant pandas usually only eat bamboo. To help them grasp the stems, they have an extra pad on their front paws that works like a thumb. Giant pandas have become rare since their forests have been cut down and because they were once hunted for their fur.

▷ Red pandas look very much like raccoons. They live in the high forests of the Himalayas, from Nepal to China. They feed at night on roots, acorns, bamboo and fruits.

Find out more
Bear
Mammal
Polar bear
Raccoon

Parrot

Parrots live in warm, tropical places around the world. They have strong, hooked beaks for cracking nuts and seeds. Each foot has two pairs of toes, which helps the birds to perch and to grip food.

▷ Macaws are brilliantly coloured parrots from South America. They are large, noisy birds and their piercing screams can often be heard in tropical rainforests.

△ Cockatoos are parrots found in Australia. This sulphur-crested cockatoo has a crest that it can raise and lower. Cockatoos are popular as pets, and often learn to copy human speech.

▷ Lovebirds are brightly coloured small parrots from Africa and Madagascar. They get their name from the way they sit together in pairs, resting their heads against each other.

Find out more
Bird
Hummingbird
Peacock

Peacock

The peacock is one of the world's most beautiful birds. Peacocks first lived in Asia but, because of their colourful feathers, they have been kept in parks and gardens for thousands of years. They have a loud piercing cry and eat snails, frogs, insects and plants.

▽ Peacocks have shiny green or blue tail feathers, tipped with a pattern like an eye. To attract females, they raise their tails and vibrate them.

▽ The female is called a peahen. Peahens have short tails, and much duller feathers than the males.

Fact box

• Peacocks have the longest tail feathers of any bird – over 1.5m.
• In 1936, a hunt started for the African Congo peacock when a single feather was discovered. The bird itself was finally found 23 years later.

▽ Pheasants are members of the same family as peacocks. Male pheasants also have long, decorative tails and brightly patterned feathers. Pheasants originally came from the Far East, but have been bred in many countries for hunting.

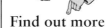

Find out more

Bird
Chicken and Turkey

Pelican

There is a rhyme about the pelican – "its beak can hold more than its belly can" – and this is true. The pelican's beak has a huge pouch which holds three times as much as its stomach. It uses the pouch to scoop up fish from the water.

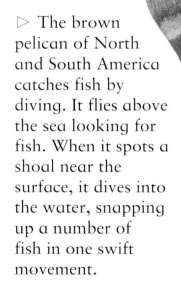

▷ Pelicans bring fish back for their young in their throats. The baby pelicans reach down into the throat to take the fish.

▷ The brown pelican of North and South America catches fish by diving. It flies above the sea looking for fish. When it spots a shoal near the surface, it dives into the water, snapping up a number of fish in one swift movement.

◁ American white pelicans use teamwork to catch fish. One group will guide the fish into shallow water by paddling their feet and moving their beaks. Once the fish are trapped, the other birds plunge their beaks in to scoop them up.

Find out more
Flamingo, Heron and Stork
Penguin

Penguin

Penguins are sea birds that live in some of the world's coldest places. They are found on islands in the seas around Antarctica, and on the southern tips of South America, South Africa and Australia. Penguins cannot fly, but they can swim better than any other bird.

△ Penguins swim using their small, stiff wings like flippers. Their tails and feet are used for steering. They hunt fish and krill, a type of shrimp. Waterproof feathers and layers of fat keep them warm.

◁ The Adélie penguin of the Antarctic islands lives in big, noisy colonies. When calling to attract a mate or to warn off other penguins, they throw back their heads.

△ Emperor penguins do not make nests. Instead, the male keeps the egg warm by balancing it on his feet. When the chick hatches it huddles close to its parent's body for the first few weeks.

◁ While the emperor penguin (above) can be up to 120 centimetres tall, the smallest penguin is the fairy penguin, which reaches a height of just 40 centimetres.

Find out more
Baby animal
Ostrich, Emu and
Cassowary
Seal and Sea lion

Physics

Physics is the study of how the universe works, and how and why things happen in it. People who study physics are called physicists. They study things such as why objects move when they are pushed, how electricity works and why things melt when they are heated. Some physicists try to find out what happens inside atoms and what the universe is made of.

△ Physicists make important discoveries. About 300 years ago, Italian scientist Galileo dropped objects from the Tower of Pisa to show that heavy things do not fall faster than light ones.

Mechanics This is the study of how things move.

Electricity Physicists study how electricity works.

Optics Studying optics means finding out about light.

Energy Physicists study how energy makes things happen.

Sound Physicists study how sound travels from place to place.

Heat Studying heat means finding out about melting, boiling and how things get hot or cold.

mechanics

mechanics

sound

optics

optics

energy

electricity

heat (and cold)

Find out more
Light and Lenses
Melting and Boiling
Motion

Pig

Pigs were first tamed 9,000 years ago in China. Today most pigs are farm animals, raised for their meat and skins. Pigs eat almost anything. They are intelligent animals and some people keep them as pets.

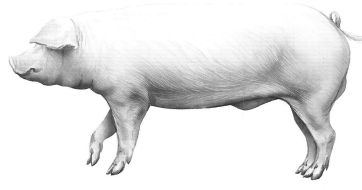

△ There are over 90 breeds of tame pig. They grow very quickly and, when raised on a special diet, may grow to two metres in length in just two years.

△▷ Baby pigs are called piglets. The mother pig, called a sow, usually has a litter of up to 12, and has two rows of teats along her belly for them to drink milk from. Sometimes the weakest piglet, called a runt, is not able to feed and needs to be looked after by a human.

▽ Wild boars are fierce animals that live in forests in many countries. The piglets have stripy coats that help to camouflage them.

Find out more
Camouflage
Goat
Mammal

Planets

Planets are huge balls of rock, metal and gas that travel around a star. Earth is one of the nine planets that travel around our star, the Sun. The Sun, and all of the planets, moons and lumps of rock, dust and ice that whirl around it, make up the Solar System. Earth only has one moon travelling around it, but some planets have several.

Earth

Sun

orbit

△ The planets travel around the Sun in fixed paths, called orbits. Earth takes one year, or just over 365 days, to orbit the Sun.

Fact box

• Mercury is the closest planet to the Sun.

• Venus is the hottest planet. It is covered with thick clouds of poisonous gas.

• Earth is the only planet with air and water.

• Mars is a red, rocky planet. It is very dry and has dust storms.

Jupiter

Earth

Mars

Mercury

Venus

Sun

Fact box

• Uranus orbits the Sun tipped on its side.

• Jupiter is the biggest planet. Its red spot is a giant whirlpool about the same size as Earth.

• Saturn has the brightest rings of all the planets. It has at least 18 moons orbiting it.

Pluto

Uranus

Neptune

Fact box

• Saturn, Jupiter, Uranus and Neptune are giant planets and are all made of gas and liquid.

• Freezing winds rip across Neptune's blue surface.

• Pluto is the coldest, smallest planet. It is the farthest away from the Sun.

Saturn

Find out more

Earth

Inventions

Moon

Space exploration

Sun

Universe

Plants

Plants grow all over the world. The biggest plants are trees and the smallest are so tiny that they can hardly be seen. Without plants, people and animals would not be able to live. They need plants for food. They also need to breathe the oxygen which comes from plants. Plants use the carbon dioxide that people and animals breathe out.

△ Most plants can make food from air, sunlight and water. They take in water through their roots.

▽ Edelweiss grows in snowy places. It has hairs on its stalks and leaves that trap heat to protect it from the cold.

edelweiss

giant saguaro cactus

yellow iris

△ A giant saguaro cactus can live for over 200 years. It survives in the hot, dry desert because it stores water in its thick stem.

white water lily   **milfoil**   **frogbit**   **water soldier**

◁ Some plants that grow in water have strong roots to anchor them in the soft mud. Others just float in the water.

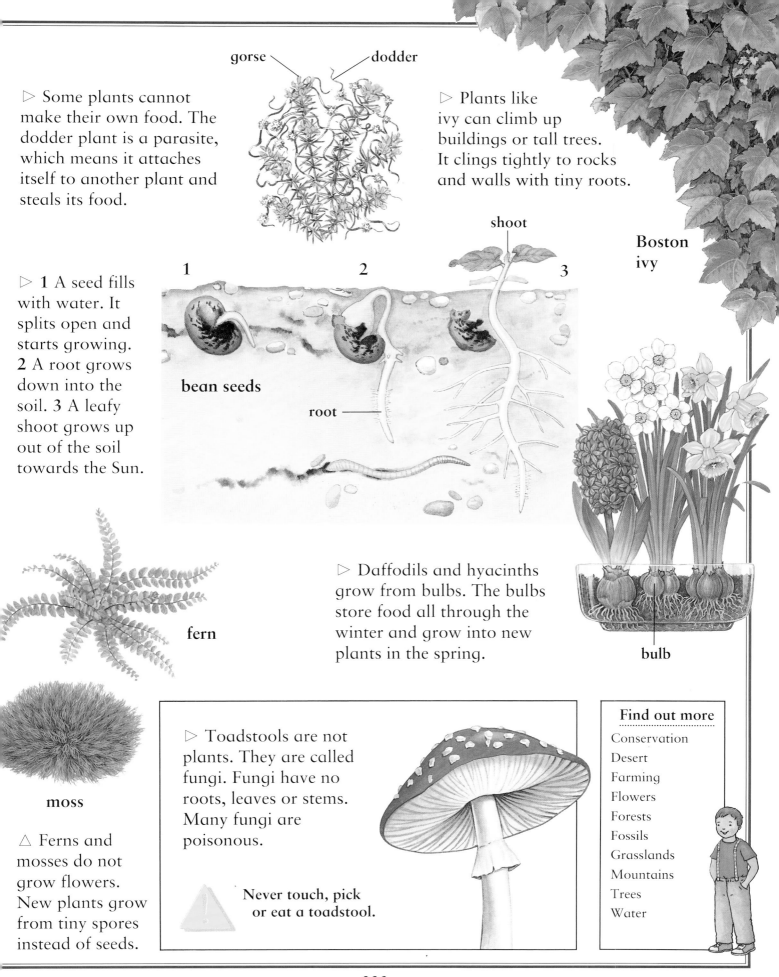

gorse   dodder

▷ Some plants cannot make their own food. The dodder plant is a parasite, which means it attaches itself to another plant and steals its food.

▷ Plants like ivy can climb up buildings or tall trees. It clings tightly to rocks and walls with tiny roots.

Boston ivy

shoot

▷ **1** A seed fills with water. It splits open and starts growing. **2** A root grows down into the soil. **3** A leafy shoot grows up out of the soil towards the Sun.

1   **2**   **3**

bean seeds

root

fern

▷ Daffodils and hyacinths grow from bulbs. The bulbs store food all through the winter and grow into new plants in the spring.

bulb

moss

△ Ferns and mosses do not grow flowers. New plants grow from tiny spores instead of seeds.

▷ Toadstools are not plants. They are called fungi. Fungi have no roots, leaves or stems. Many fungi are poisonous.

Never touch, pick or eat a toadstool.

Find out more

Conservation
Desert
Farming
Flowers
Forests
Fossils
Grasslands
Mountains
Trees
Water

Platypus

The platypus is a strange animal. It has a beaver's tail, a duck's bill and webbed feet. Like a reptile, it lays eggs, but it also gives milk to its young, just as mammals do. It belongs to a small group of animals called monotremes, which have features of both mammals and reptiles.

Fact box
• The only other monotremes are the spiny anteaters of New Guinea and Australia.
• The platypus grows to be 60cm long.
• Each adult platypus lives alone in its own burrow.

△ The platypus is found in Australia and Tasmania. Like the otter, the platypus lives in a burrow and hunts in the water.

◁ The platypus has fur similar to an otter's. Even its flat tail is covered in fur. When swimming, the platypus paddles with its front feet and steers with its back feet and tail. It uses its sensitive, rubbery bill to find food in the muddy beds of the rivers and lakes where it lives. Platypuses eat crayfish, shrimp, worms, frogs and small fish. They are greedy animals and eat their own weight in food every day.

▷ Before laying her eggs, the female platypus makes a nest at the end of her burrow. She lays two or three eggs, then seals the opening of the tunnel to stop predators entering.

Find out more
Beaver
Otter
Shrimp and Prawn

Polar bear

Polar bears live in the frozen regions of the Arctic, where they hunt and raise their young. Their white fur makes them almost invisible in the snow. They mainly feed on seals, but also eat fish, geese and ducks. They are the only northern bears that do not hibernate in the winter.

△ Polar bears have thick, oily coats and a layer of fat to protect them from the icy temperatures, which can drop to –30°C.

◁ Polar bears are good swimmers – they have to be to cross the moving packs of ice. They are often found swimming in the sea many kilometres away from an ice pack or land. Their large, furry feet make good paddles for swimming.

△ Polar bears often wait at the breathing holes of seals. When the seal comes up for air, the bear catches it, kills it and then eats it.

Fact box

• Male polar bears weigh up to 800 kilograms.
• Baby polar bears are born in early December in ice dens. They stay in these with their mothers until spring.

◁ Polar bears live alone and only meet when they go south to mate. They go as far as the mouth of the Amur River in Russia and the Gulf of St. Lawrence in Canada.

Find out more
Bear
Penguin
Seal and Sea lion

Prehistoric life

Earth is thousands of millions of years old. When it was first formed, there was no life at all. The first animals grew in the sea. Since then, millions of different kinds of animals have lived on Earth. We know what some of them looked like from the fossils of their remains.

Earth was formed 4,600 million years ago.

the first living things appeared in the sea 3,500 million years ago

the first amphibians lived 370 million years ago

Ichthyostega
(Ik-thee-o-stee-ga)

△ Ichthyostega was one of the very first amphibians. It lived on land and water.

all the dinosaurs became extinct 65 million years ago

▽ Dinosaurs died out 65 million years ago. Since life began on Earth, millions of animals have died out to be replaced by new animals.

the first humans lived two million years ago

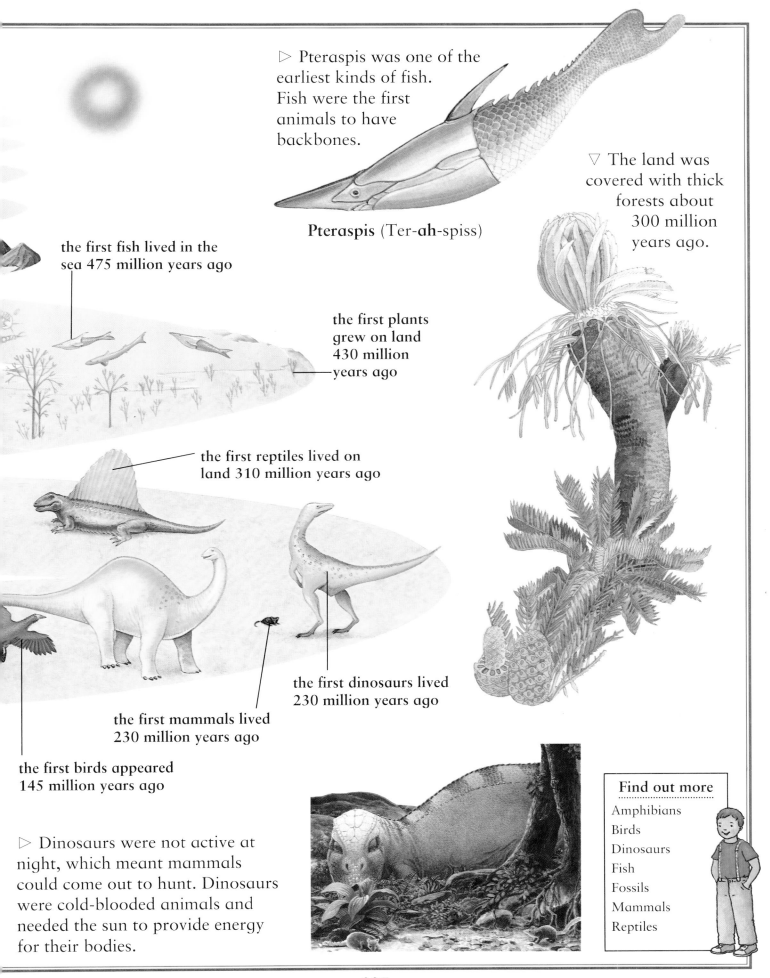

▷ Pteraspis was one of the earliest kinds of fish. Fish were the first animals to have backbones.

Pteraspis (Ter-**ah**-spiss)

▽ The land was covered with thick forests about 300 million years ago.

the first fish lived in the sea 475 million years ago

the first plants grew on land 430 million years ago

the first reptiles lived on land 310 million years ago

the first dinosaurs lived 230 million years ago

the first mammals lived 230 million years ago

the first birds appeared 145 million years ago

▷ Dinosaurs were not active at night, which meant mammals could come out to hunt. Dinosaurs were cold-blooded animals and needed the sun to provide energy for their bodies.

Find out more
Amphibians
Birds
Dinosaurs
Fish
Fossils
Mammals
Reptiles

Rabbit and Hare

Rabbits and hares are closely related. Hares are bigger than rabbits and have longer ears and legs. Hares live aboveground, while rabbits live underground in linked-up tunnels, called warrens.

△ The black-tailed jack rabbit of the hot North American deserts is really a hare. Its very long ears help it to cool down in the fierce heat of the day.

△ Rabbits were originally found in the countries around the Mediterranean Sea. Humans have now introduced them throughout the world.

▽ Rabbits are popular pets. They are friendly animals and easy to keep in outdoor hutches. They need to be fed and watered every day and their hutches must be cleaned regularly.

Fact box
• Rabbits have up to ten babies in a litter and give birth seven times a year.
• Young hares are called leverets.
• Top speed for a hare is 56 kilometres per hour.

Find out more
Guinea pig, Gerbil and Hamster
Rat
Squirrel

Raccoon

The striped tail and black mask of the North American raccoon make it easy to spot. Raccoons are forest creatures, but they have learned to scavenge from humans and often make their dens near towns.

△ People's rubbish makes a tasty lunch for a raccoon. Raccoons will often get used to humans and can be partly tamed. However, they will always keep their wild instincts and may be fierce fighters.

△ Even though they are weaned at two months, young raccoons are protected by their mother for up to a year.

▷ In the wild, raccoons eat berries, acorns and seeds. They like to live near rivers so they can hunt for crabs, frogs and fish. They will also rinse any dirty food in the water. When the young are old enough, they will leave their mother to live on their own.

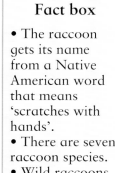

Fact box

• The raccoon gets its name from a Native American word that means 'scratches with hands'.
• There are seven raccoon species.
• Wild raccoons live for about five years.

Find out more
Bear
Beaver
Fox
Panda

Radio

Radio is a way of sending messages over long distances. Sounds are turned into waves, called radio waves. These travel from one place to another through air and space. You cannot see them because they are invisible.

Radio waves are also used to send signals from radio and television stations, and to carry messages to and from mobile telephones.

△ The aerial on a radio picks up radio waves coming from a transmitter. The radio turns the waves back into sound.

◁ In a radio station, music and other sounds are turned into an electrical signal. This signal goes to a transmitter, which turns it into radio waves.

▷ A walkie-talkie radio turns the sound of your voice into radio waves. The waves travel to another walkie-talkie radio which turns them back into sound.

△ This is a radio telescope. It picks up radio waves coming from space. Astronomers study these waves to find out things about the Universe that they cannot learn from ordinary telescopes.

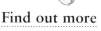

Find out more

Electricity
Microwaves
Sound
Telephones

Rat

Rats are rodents with sharp teeth, furry bodies and long tails. There are over 120 types of rat, living all over the world. The brown rat and the black rat are the most common.

△ Brown rats and black rats originally came from Asia, but they are now found all over the world, wherever humans live. It is said that there is probably one rat for every person on the planet.

△ Both black and brown female rats will have between six and 22 babies in a litter. They can have up to seven litters a year.

▷ Pack rats, also called wood rats, are American rodents that live in nests made of plants. They are nocturnal and eat grasses and cereals.

Fact box

• Rats can carry about 30 diseases affecting humans.
• In the Middle Ages, one in four Europeans died from the plague – a disease spread by rats.
• Rats have been known to gnaw through electric cables!

▷ Humans see rats as pests because they spread disease and spoil human foods. They are intelligent animals and will use their sharp teeth to bite through most obstacles.

Find out more
Beaver
Guinea pig, Gerbil and Hamster
Mouse

Rattlesnake

Rattlesnakes are found in North and South America. They are named after their spooky rattle, which warns other animals that they are very poisonous. There are about 30 species of rattlesnake.

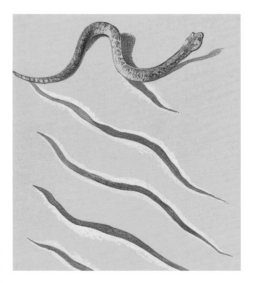

◁ The sidewinder is a rattlesnake that lives in sandy deserts in Mexico and the southwestern United States. Its unusual method of moving sideways leaves a distinctive trail.

△ Most rattlesnakes rest during the day and hunt small rodents at night. They detect prey by 'tasting' the air for smells with their forked tongue. As the prey moves closer the rattlesnake feels its body warmth with heat-sensitive pits on the sides of its face.

Fact box
• At 2.5m long, the eastern diamondback is the biggest rattlesnake.
• A rattlesnake's poison comes out of two fangs in its upper jaw.
• The bite of a rattlesnake can be deadly.

▷ Inside a rattlesnake's tail is a set of hard, loose pieces. It is these that produce the rattling noise. You can make your own rattle by threading some bottle tops onto a long nail and attaching it to a length of wood (get an adult to help you). You might scare a few people!

Find out more
Cobra
Reptile

Recording

Recording something means storing it in a way that makes it possible to see or hear it again and again. We can record voices, music and pictures.

When we talk about recording, we usually mean recording sound. What we actually record are vibrations in the air. We can do this with a tape recorder.

△ **1** When you record your voice, a microphone turns sound (vibrations in the air) into an electrical signal. The signal is recorded on the tape in the tape recorder.

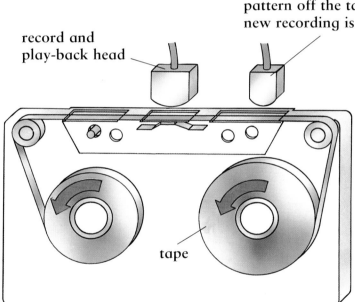

this head wipes the magnetic pattern off the tape before a new recording is made

record and play-back head

tape

◁ **2** The tape in a tape recorder has a special magnetic coating. When a recording is being made, an electromagnet in the recorder makes an invisible pattern on the tape.

Fact box

• Many aircraft have flight recorders that record the aircraft's movements during a flight. A cockpit voice recorder records what the pilots say during the flight as well.

△**3** To play a recording, the tape recorder turns the invisible patterns into an electrical signal. This signal goes to a loudspeaker, which turns it into sound.

▷ On a compact disc (CD), sounds are recorded as a pattern of tiny pits in the surface. A laser beam in the player reads this pattern and the electronics inside the player turn it into sound.

Find out more
Electricity
Magnets
Sound
Video

Reindeer

Reindeer are found in the Arctic regions of Asia, Europe and North America. They live on the tundra (plains) and in forests. The reindeer is closely related to the caribou of North America.

▽ Like all other deer, reindeer lose their antlers in spring, then grow a new set that reaches full size in autumn. Reindeer are the only deer where the females have antlers as well as males.

△ Reindeer feed on grass, lichens and twigs. In the winter they use their large hooves to shovel the snow away to dig for food. In winter their thick coats are grey; in summer they are brown.

▽ People first tamed the reindeer over 3,000 years ago, and they have been used as transport and for their meat and fur ever since. Humans have never managed to tame the caribou.

◁ Reindeer and caribou migrate over long distances. They move south in the autumn and north in the spring. Young or weak animals are often preyed on by hungry wolves.

Find out more
Deer
Elk
Mammal
Migration

Religion

There are many religions around the world and the people who follow them have different beliefs and customs. Most religions have a god or gods and have rules to tell people how to live together. People who follow a religion may say prayers in a special building and have a priest to guide them. The most popular religions in the world are Christianity, Islam, Hinduism, Buddhism, Sikhism and Judaism.

church

△ Many people worship in special buildings. They may pray in a church, like this one, a mosque, a temple or a synagogue.

Christians
These Christians are celebrating Easter Sunday. They believe that Jesus, the Son of God, died on the cross and came back to life at Easter. They follow his teachings that are written in the New Testament of the Bible.

Sikhs

The Golden Temple at Amritsar in India is the most important holy place where Sikhs go to pray. Sikhs believe in one God and follow the teachings of gurus. They are taught to lead good, simple lives.

Hindus

Every year Hindus celebrate Divali, the festival of lights, to bring good fortune. They worship many gods and believe the soul is re-born after death.

Jews

Candles are lit in a special candlestick during the Jewish festival of Hanukkah. Jews believe in God and their teachings and laws are written in the Bible.

Buddhists

Buddhists say their prayers in front of statues of Buddha, like this one. They follow the teachings of an Indian prince who became known as Buddha.

Muslims

Followers of Islam are called Muslims. These Muslims are praying in the holy city of Mecca. They believe in one God, called Allah, whose words were written down by Muhammad in the Koran.

Other religions

There are many other religions each with their own festivals. Some worship the spirits of natural things, such as trees and rocks. This is a fishing festival in Japan.

Find out more

Asia
Books
Dance
Europe
History
North America
South America

Reproduction

Plants make seeds that grow into new plants. Animals have babies that grow into adults. This is called reproduction. It means making new plants and animals that live on when their parents die. Usually, two plants or animals, one female and one male, are needed for reproduction.

△ For a plant to make seeds, a male flower's pollen has to join with a female flower's ovary. Some plants have both male and female flowers. Others need insects to carry pollen from flower to flower. These flowers are bee-shaped to attract bees to their pollen.

Fact box
• Some fish lay millions of eggs. This way they make sure that some, at least, survive and grow.
• Blue whales have the biggest young of all animals. A newborn baby weighs 5 tonnes.

▷ This foal is drinking milk from its mother. The milk contains everything the foal needs to grow strong and healthy. Horses are mammals. All mammal mothers produce milk for their young at the start of their lives.

amoeba

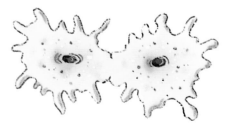

△ Some living things are very small and simple. They are made up of just one cell. Instead of having young, they reproduce by splitting in two.

baby in womb

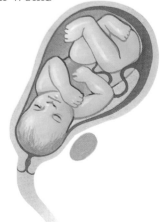

◁ Before you were born, you spent nine months growing inside your mother's womb. You grew from two tiny cells, an egg from your mother and a sperm cell from your father.

△ Amphibians reproduce in water. A female frog, for example, lays hundreds of eggs in the water. Then the male fertilises (adds his sperm to) them.

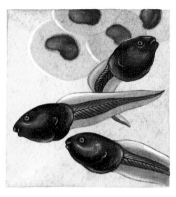

△ Tadpoles form inside the eggs and then hatch out. They do not look like frogs, yet. They look more like fish.

△ Gradually, the tadpoles grow legs and lose their tails.

△ This young frog is now ready to leave the water.

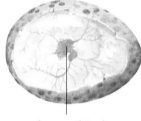

embryo (bird beginning to form)

◁ 1 Female birds lay eggs. The egg has a hard shell to protect the baby growing inside. It also has a store of food in its yolk.

▽ This is a seed beginning to grow into a new plant. It grows roots first, then a shoot and then leaves.

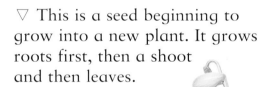

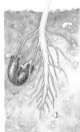

▷ 2 The parent birds sit on the egg to keep it warm as the baby bird grows inside.

young bird growing

▷ 3 At last, the baby bird is ready to hatch. It pecks at the shell to break it, and then squeezes out.

young bird

Find out more

Flight
Human body
Living things
Water

Reptiles

Lizards, crocodiles, turtles and snakes are all reptiles. Some reptiles live in water and some live on land.

Most reptiles live in warm countries. Reptiles that live in cold places sleep through the winter. This is called hibernation. They wake up in the spring when the weather is warmer.

△ Most snakes lay eggs with soft, leathery shells. The young snakes hatch when the eggs are warmed by the heat of the Sun.

gecko

△ A gecko is a lizard with sticky pads on its toes. The pads allow it to run upside down across a ceiling.

◁ A crocodile mother looks after her young. When the babies hatch, their mother carries them carefully to the water in her enormous mouth.

Nile crocodile

Fact box

• All reptiles are cold-blooded. This means that they have to lie in the sun to warm up before they can move around. If their bodies get too hot they have to cool down in the shade.

• Reptiles have dry, scaly skin.

• Dinosaurs were reptiles. The word dinosaur means terrible lizard.

▷ The frilled lizard spreads its collar and hisses loudly to frighten away enemies.

frilled lizard

green turtle

◁ A turtle swims using its strong flippers. It lives in the sea, but it lays its eggs on the seashore.

▽ Many snakes have stretchy jaws, so they can open their mouths very wide. Some snakes can eat a large animal by swallowing it whole.

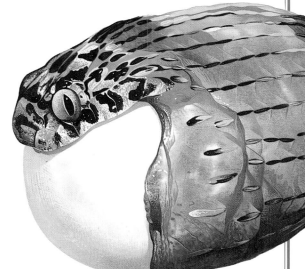

egg-eating snake

▷ The tortoise lives on land. It pulls its head and legs into its shell if it is scared.

tortoise

▽ The anaconda is a huge snake. It coils its body around its prey and squeezes it to death.

caiman

anaconda

▽ A Komodo dragon is the largest lizard. It can grow up to three and a half metres long. It attacks deer and pigs.

Komodo dragon

Find out more

Animals
Dinosaurs
Prehistoric life

Rhinoceros

Rhinoceroses (or rhinos) are large, heavy animals that live on open grassland in Asia and Africa. They are protected from predators by tough, armoured skin and sharp horns. Although rhino horn is very hard, it is actually made of a material similar to hair.

△ Rhinos weigh up to five tonnes and can charge at 50 kilometres per hour.

▽ Rhinos have poor eyesight, but a very good sense of smell. Females with young calves are likely to charge if they feel threatened by an unfamiliar sound or scent, and males are often bad-tempered. But rhinos will let birds called oxpeckers ride on their backs and feed on insects living on the rhino's skin.

Indian rhino   African white rhino   African black rhino

△ African rhinos have two horns; Asian rhinos have one. Indian rhinos have a long upper lip for eating reeds and grass. The white rhino, which is actually grey, has a wide upper lip for grazing. The black rhino uses its pointed upper lip to eat leaves.

Find out more
Elephant
Hippopotamus
Horse
Pig

Roads

Roads link one place to another. Cars, buses and lorries travel on roads. Very large roads are called motorways. They have no crossroads or roundabouts, so traffic can travel a long way without stopping. Signs and markings on roads tell drivers which way to go and how fast to travel.

△ Bridges and flyovers help traffic to travel more quickly around crowded cities. Some roads go underground, through tunnels.

How a road is made
▷ Bulldozers shovel away trees and earth.

bulldozer

◁ Scrapers make the ground level and smooth out a path. Scrapers are pulled by very large tractors.

scraper

dumptruck

grader

◁ Dumptrucks bring crushed rock. Graders smooth this in place to make a flat base for the road.

roller

paving machine

△ A paving machine spreads on a mixture of stones, sand and tar, called asphalt. This is then rolled.

Find out more
Conservation
Energy

Salmon and Trout

Salmon and some kinds of trout are found in the cold northern parts of the Atlantic and Pacific Oceans. Most types of trout, however, live in fresh water. Large salmon can weigh up to 30 kilograms, while the largest trout weigh over 13.5 kilograms.

△ There are many different types of trout. The brightly coloured rainbow trout (above) is one of the most common. It was introduced to Europe from North America and people often catch it for sport.

▽ Before they breed, salmon migrate thousands of kilometres from their homes in the sea, back to the rivers where they were born. They battle upstream against strong currents, clearing obstacles such as waterfalls by leaping up to 3.5 metres high.

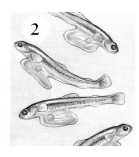

△ **1** The female salmon makes a small hole in the gravel on the riverbed and lays her eggs. The male then fertilizes them. **2** At birth, young salmon have a pouch on their sides that contains food.

▽ **3** After a year the young salmon develop red stripes on their sides. **4** By the time they are 15 centimetres long, the salmon are silver coloured. They are now ready to journey down the river to the sea, where they will grow into adults and repeat the cycle.

Find out more
Fish
Migration
Reproduction

Satellites

A satellite is an object in space that travels around another object, such as a planet. This is called being in orbit. The Moon is a natural satellite that has orbited the Earth for billions of years. The other satellites orbiting the Earth are made by people. They are launched into orbit by space rockets. Some watch and measure the weather, some are used for communications and some investigate outer space.

Communications satellites can carry telephone messages through space to the other side of the world. A message is beamed up from Earth to the satellite and then back down again to a receiver, which can be thousands of kilometres away from the caller.

▽ This satellite looks for cosmic rays. Its solar panels turn sunlight into electricity that the satellite needs to work. Its aerial sends information back to Earth. It also has thrusters, like tiny rockets, that turn the satellite to point in different directions.

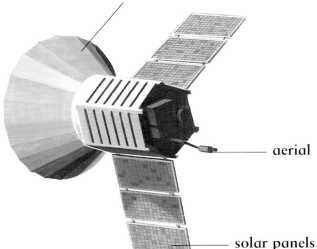

radiation detector

aerial

solar panels

signals

◁ The Hubble space telescope is a satellite that takes pictures of objects far out in space and sends them back to Earth. This picture shows the space shuttle (and re-useable space rocket) putting the telescope into orbit high above the Earth.

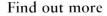

Find out more

Energy
Radio
Solar System
Telephones
Universe
Weather

Science

Scientists study the world around us. Biologists study living things, geologists study the Earth and astronomers study the stars and planets. All scientists look at things and try to explain what they see. They set up experiments to test their ideas. Scientists discover new things all the time.

leaf under microscope

△ A microscope makes things look much larger. Scientists use all sorts of tools to help them understand the world around us.

sinks   floats

◁ You can be a scientist too. These children are doing an experiment. First they guess which objects might float and which will sink. They sort them into piles.

floats

sinks

◁ They drop the things from each pile into a tank of water to see if their guess was right. They think of reasons why some objects float and others sink. Do you know the reasons why?

Find out more

Antarctica and Arctic

Electricity

Scorpion

Scorpions are part of the same group of animals as spiders – the arachnids. They have eight legs, two powerful claws and a stinging tail. Scorpions hide by day and only come out at night.

stinging tail

claw

▷ Scorpions catch their prey in their claws and use the sting in their tail to kill it. The sting is also used in defence against predators like mongooses. Most scorpion stings are similar to those of a wasp, but some are strong enough to kill humans.

▽ Female scorpions keep their eggs inside their bodies until they are ready to hatch. When the young scorpions are born, they climb onto their mother's back.

△ Male scorpions may fight over a mate, wrestling with their claws and trying to sting each other. Before mating, the male and female also grapple in a complicated dance.

Find out more

Spider

Sea bird

Some birds spend all their lives near the sea, eating fish and nesting on cliffs or beaches. These birds are well adapted to life near the ocean: they usually have webbed feet for swimming, a sharp bill for catching fish and waterproof feathers.

◁ **1** Sea birds need waterproof feathers so they do not get soggy and sink. Squirt water at a sea bird feather and you will see how the natural oils on the feather repel the water.

△ Gannets are large, white sea birds with black-tipped wings. They fly above the surface of the water until they spot a shoal of fish. Then they dive deep into the sea.

▷ **2** Take an even closer look at the feather with a magnifying glass. Can you see how the barbs link together? This flat surface is called the vane.

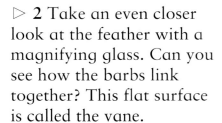

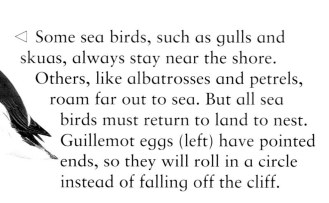

◁ Some sea birds, such as gulls and skuas, always stay near the shore. Others, like albatrosses and petrels, roam far out to sea. But all sea birds must return to land to nest. Guillemot eggs (left) have pointed ends, so they will roll in a circle instead of falling off the cliff.

Find out more
Albatross
Bird
Fish
Gull
Pelican
Penguin

Sea cow

The dugong and the manatee are sea cows. They are mammals that live in warm tropical seas, feeding on sea grass and water plants. The dugong is found in the Indian and Pacific Oceans. The manatee lives in the tropical waters of America, the West Indies and Africa.

△ The dugong has a V-shaped tail. Adults grow to be 3.4 metres long. Unlike the manatee, male dugongs grow two tusk-like teeth.

Fact box

• Female sea cows give birth to one baby at a time.
• Sea cows suckle their babies at teats on their chest. They can hold the baby to a teat with a flipper.
• Amazonian manatees gather in groups of 500.

▽ Manatees have round tails, shaped like paddles. They swim slowly and have bad eyesight.

△ Sea cows may live alone or in small groups. They seem to be affectionate animals – manatees often greet each other by touching noses, which looks as if they are kissing.

△ In the 18th century, sailors used to kill manatees for food. Manatees are now a protected species, but they are sometimes injured by boat propellers while swimming in shallow water.

Find out more
Dolphin
Seal and Sea lion
Walrus

Seahorse

Seahorses are fish that live in warm seas. Because they swim upright and are covered by bony armour, they do not look like fish. However, they are related to the stickleback.

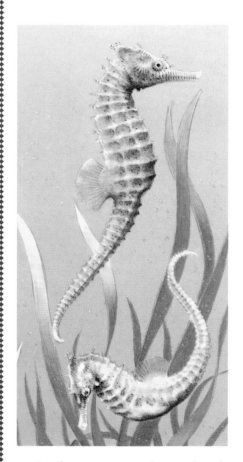

△ Seahorses spend much of their lives anchored by their tails to seaweed. They feed on shrimps and plankton, which they suck into their long mouths.

▷ When seahorses mate, the male and female meet belly to belly and the female lays her eggs in a pouch on the male. Five weeks later, up to 200 young hatch from his body, looking just like tiny adults.

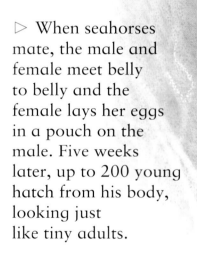

◁ The sea dragon is a type of seahorse found around the coasts of Australia. It is 1.5 metres long and is camouflaged by leafy-looking growths all over its body.

Find out more
Camouflage
Coral reef
Fish
Reproduction

Seal and Sea lion

Seals and sea lions are good swimmers and divers. They are mammals so they have to come up to breathe, but they can stay underwater for up to 30 minutes. They feed on fish and penguins.

▽ While sea lions can walk on their flippers, seals cannot. Male sea lions have thick fur on their necks that looks like the mane of a lion.

▽ Seals catch their prey underwater, then they come to the surface to eat it.

◁ Female seals and sea lions suckle (feed) their babies on milk that is extremely nourishing. The milk is full of fat and helps the babies grow quickly.

▽ Male elephant seals are the largest seals in the world. They get their name from their floppy noses, which look like trunks.

Fact box

• The Baikal seal of Russia is the only freshwater seal in the world.
• Sea lion colonies sometimes have hundreds of thousands of sea lions in them.
• Monk seals are one of the few species to live in tropical water, such as the Caribbean Sea.

Find out more

Dolphin
Killer whale
Penguin

Seashore

The seashore is where the land meets the sea. Some seashores are sandy, others may be rocky, muddy or pebbly. Many different animals and plants live there. The seashore changes its shape all the time. This is because the waves pound against the cliffs and beaches, slowly wearing them away.

△ Many seabirds live on the cliffs at the seaside. Puffins nest in burrows at the top. Gannets nest at the top of the cliff too and on ledges below.

puffin

gannet

△ Twice a day the sea comes high up the shore. This is called high tide.

△ The sea also falls back again twice every day. This is called low tide.

◁ Playing on the beach can be great fun. Sand is made up of very tiny pieces of broken rock and shell.

Always use sun cream and a hat to shade yourself from the sun's harmful rays.

Find out more
Animals
Birds
Caves
Europe
Fossils
Oceans and Seas

Seasons

Many parts of the world have four seasons. They are spring, summer, autumn and winter. This is because the Earth is tilted as it travels around the Sun. As the Earth circles the Sun, either the northern half or the southern half of the world leans towards the Sun.

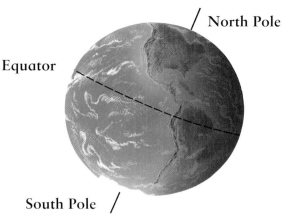

North Pole

Equator

South Pole

△ It is summer in the southern part of the world when it faces the Sun. In the northern part it is winter.

◁ Spring follows winter. The days become longer and warmer. Plants begin to grow and many animals have babies.

◁ Summer is the warmest season. Flowers bloom and fruits ripen in the sunshine. It does not get dark until late.

◁ In autumn the days get shorter. The weather turns cooler. Trees may lose their leaves. Some birds fly to warmer places.

△ It is always hot near the Equator. Often there is a dry season and a wet season.

◁ Winter is the coldest season. It gets dark early in the evening. Plants stop growing and many trees are bare.

Find out more

Antarctica and Arctic

Birds

Plants

Trees

Weather

Senses

How do you know what is happening around you, or what something feels like or smells like? The answer is that you use your senses. Humans have five senses. These are sight, hearing, touch, taste and smell. We often use more than one sense at a time. For example, when you eat something, you smell and taste it at the same time – and see it, too.

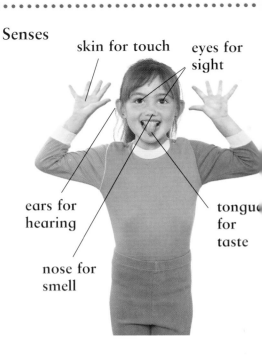

skin for touch

eyes for sight

ears for hearing

tongue for taste

nose for smell

▷ **1** Get a friend to guess what something is just by using his or her sense of touch. Cut a hole in the side of a large cardboard box. Make it big enough to put an arm through. Find a few different objects to put in the box.

△ Your sense organs pick up tastes, touches, smells, sounds and sights. They send messages about these along your nerves to your brain. Your brain sorts these messages out and tells you what is going on around you.

Fact box

• Not everyone's senses work in the same way. For example, there are people who cannot easily tell red and green colours apart. This is because the light-sensitive cells in their eyes do not work properly.

△ **2** Do not let your friend see what the objects are. Can your friend tell what each one is just by feeling it through the hole?

△ Can you see the line of dots along the side of this fish? They act like another pair of eyes and detect movements made by other creatures nearby in the water. This helps the fish to find food and to escape from enemies.

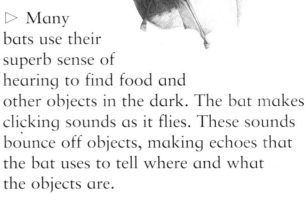

▷ Many bats use their superb sense of hearing to find food and other objects in the dark. The bat makes clicking sounds as it flies. These sounds bounce off objects, making echoes that the bat uses to tell where and what the objects are.

▽ One boy bursts a balloon, and the other boy points to where the sound is coming from. He hears the sound more loudly in one ear than the other. This tells him where the sound is being made.

△ Dogs have a much better sense of smell than humans. This dog has been trained to use its sense of smell to search for explosives.

△ This person's sense of sight does not work properly, so her guide dog helps her to find her way around.

Find out more
Colour
Human body
Light and Lenses
Sound

Shark

Sharks are the most fearsome predators in the ocean. They are excellent hunters and find their prey either by its smell, or by tracking the tiny electrical currents that the prey's body gives out.

great white shark

hammerhead shark

△ The world's most dangerous shark is the great white. It can grow to be 12 metres long, and has a huge mouth full of sharp, pointed teeth. Great whites are found in warm waters all over the world. They sometimes attack bathers and surfers, but seals and sea lions are their favourite prey.

◁ The hammerhead shark uses its huge head to steer itself. Sharks are a kind of fish, but instead of fish scales they have rough skin, and instead of bone their skeleton is made of rubbery cartilage.

◁ At over 15 metres long, the whale shark is the largest of all fish. It eats some of the smallest creatures in the sea – plankton.

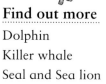

Find out more
Dolphin
Killer whale
Seal and Sea lion

Shellfish

Shellfish are water creatures whose soft bodies are protected by hard shells. Like slugs, snails and octopuses, they are molluscs. They are found in freshwater and saltwater all over the world.

△ When shellfish die, all that remains is the shell. If you go to the seaside, collect as many different shells as you can. Later, you can display them on a board with their names underneath them.

Fact box

• Some shellfish have just one shell, others have a pair.
• Shells are made from minerals. These make the shells very hard.
• Shellfish have existed on Earth for 600 million years.

◁ Most shellfish feed by filtering tiny food particles from the water. Some shellfish stay on the same rock all their lives. They anchor themselves with a single sucker foot, or by threads.

▽ Mussels have two matching shells that clamp shut when they are in danger. They hold on to rocks using threads that are so strong they can resist huge storm waves.

lambis shell   **top shell**

tiger cowrie

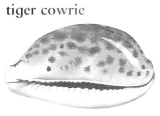

Find out more

Crab
Octopus and Squid

Ships and boats

Boats have been used for thousands of years to carry people and goods across water. The first boats were rafts, made from logs or reeds tied together. Boats use sails, oars or engines to push them through the water. Large, sea-going boats are called ships. There are many different kinds of ships and boats.

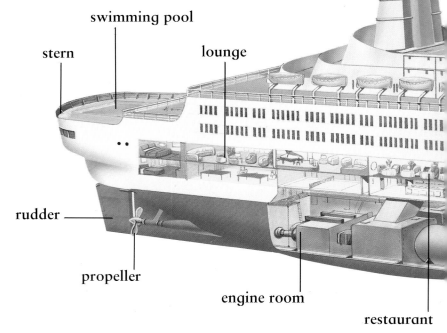

△ Long ago, the people of Polynesia explored the Pacific Ocean in boats like canoes. They were searching for new islands.

▷ Huge passenger ships are called cruise liners. They are like floating hotels. The parts of a ship all have names. The front is called the bow and the back is called the stern.

funnel

swimming pool

stern

lounge

rudder

propeller

engine room

restaurant

Viking longship

△ The Vikings were great sailors. They built strong, wooden ships, called longboats, which had square sails. They could also row their ships through the water with oars.

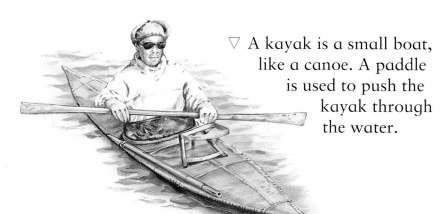

▽ A kayak is a small boat, like a canoe. A paddle is used to push the kayak through the water.

kayak

▷ A speed boat has a powerful engine. The front lifts up so it can skim quickly across the top of the water.

speed boat

▽ A racing yacht has a large sail at the front, called the spinnaker. When it catches the wind, the yacht races along the sea.

racing yacht

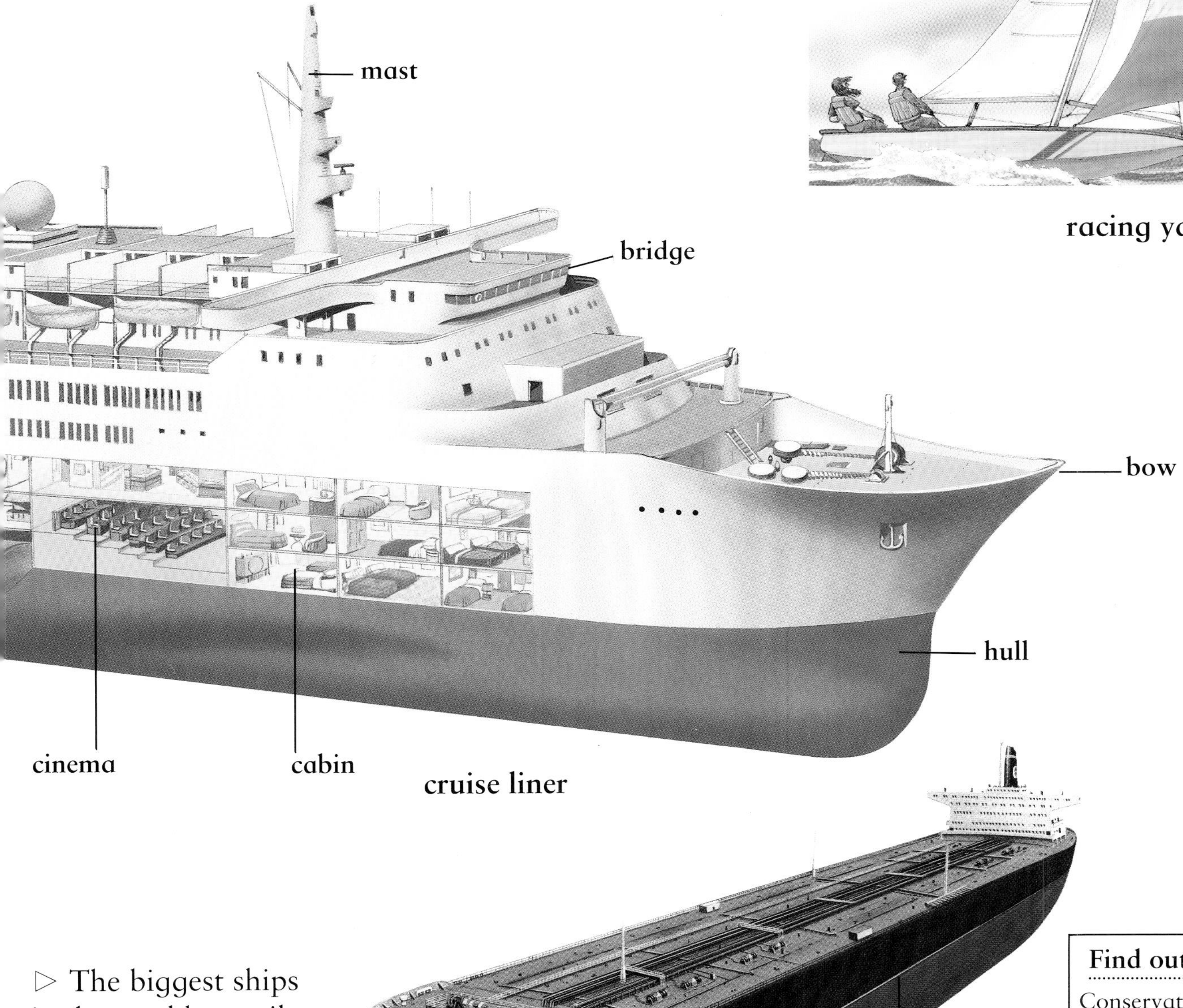

mast

bridge

bow

hull

cinema

cabin

cruise liner

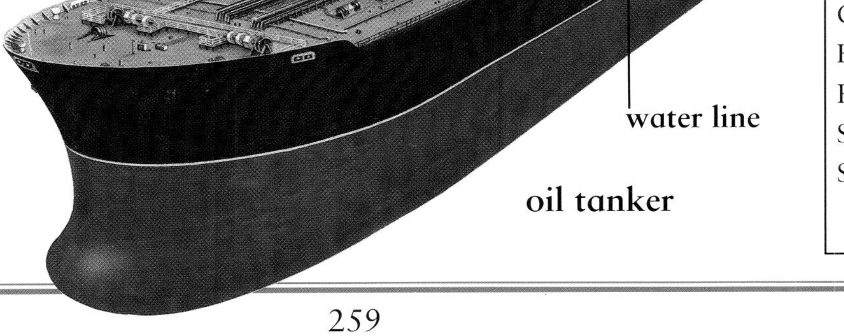

water line

▷ The biggest ships in the world are oil tankers. They can be half a kilometre long and so heavy that they take 20 minutes to stop.

oil tanker

Find out more

Conservation
History
Religion
Science
South America

Shrimp and Prawn

Shrimps and prawns live in seas, rivers and lakes almost everywhere. They are related to lobsters but are smaller and are better swimmers. Prawns are slighly bigger than shrimps.

△ The pistol shrimp, which grows to about four centimetres long, has very large claws. It snaps them together to stun its prey.

▽ **1** Make an underwater viewer to look at shrimps and prawns in rock pools. Get an adult to cut the bottom off a clear plastic bottle. Stretch cling film over the cut end and secure with an elastic band.

▽ **2** You will need to keep still, as these animals are easily frightened.

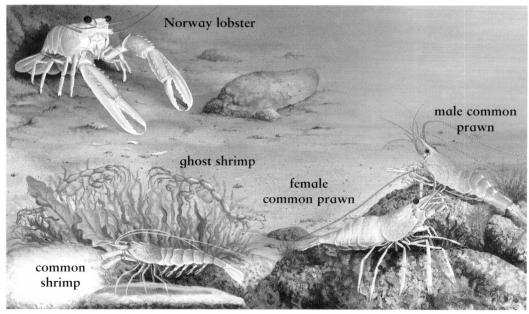

Norway lobster

ghost shrimp

female common prawn

male common prawn

common shrimp

◁ Shrimps and prawns often search for food on the seabed. They eat small plants and animals. They swim by flicking their fan-like tails.

Find out more
Crab
Shellfish

Skunk

Skunks live in woods and grassland in North and South America. They have long, furry tails and black-and-white fur. They are known for the foul smell they give off in defence.

△ Skunks have around three babies in the spring. The young are born blind and do not leave the burrow for six weeks. When fully grown, they leave to find their own home.

△ Skunks are about the size of domestic cats, and weigh up to three kilograms. They rest in their burrows by day, and come out at night to find plants, birds' eggs, insects and small mammals to eat.

▷ The skunk has a special way of dealing with a predator such as a lynx. First it thumps its paws on the ground. Then it turns round, flinging up its rear legs to expose its bottom.

Fact box

• The commonest skunk in North America is the striped skunk.
• The other two types are the hog-nosed skunk and the spotted skunk.
• Skunks can spray an attacker from a distance of 4m. The smell lasts for days.

▷ If the attacker does not heed the warning, the skunk lowers its legs and squirts a jet of liquid from glands near the tail. The smell is so awful that few predators return for more.

Find out more
Badger
Otter

Sloth

Someone who is lazy or slow might be described as being slothful. Looking at the sloth, it is easy to see why. The sloth spends its life hanging in the trees by its hooked claws, and it hardly ever moves at all.

Fact box
• Sloths are found in the rainforests of South America.
• Once every two to three weeks, they climb down to the ground to go to the toilet.
• Sloths can fall asleep in their hanging position.

▽ The female gives birth to one young, which she carries on her stomach for about five weeks after its birth. The baby sloth stays on by clinging to its mother's fur.

△ Sloths wake at night to feed on leaves and fruits. The hair on their coats hangs down from the belly to the back so the rainwater can flow off easily. Some species have algae growing in their coats. This gives them a greenish colour that camouflages them in the trees.

△ Although sloths move slowly on land, they can swim well. They are not afraid to cross large rivers and swamps to find food and new trees to live in.

Find out more
Camouflage
Mammal
Monkey

Slug and Snail

Slugs and snails are found all over the world, both on land and in water. They have feelers on their heads, soft bodies, and a single muscular foot that is also their stomach. Snails have shells but slugs do not.

◁ Watch how slugs and snails move by placing them on a piece of clear glass or plastic. You will see that they ooze a trail of slime to ease their way along.

△ Garden slugs and snails mostly feed on rotting plants. But they sometimes eat growing plants, so they can be bad for gardens. Their mouths are full of tiny teeth.

▽ Snails are known for moving slowly, but a snail race can still be very exciting. On a board, make three lanes with string held in place by pins. Chalk a line at the start and at the finish, then set them off. First past the finish is the winner.

Fact box

• Land species have lungs to breathe; water species have gills.
• The giant land snail can be 30cm long.
• Tropical cone snails feed on fish. First they paralyse them by injecting nerve poison from a tooth on the end of their tongues.

Find out more
Centipede
Fish
Habitat
Shellfish

Solar System

The Solar System is made up of the Sun and the nine planets that orbit (travel around) it. One of these planets is the Earth. Some of these planets have moons orbiting around them. Comets and asteroids whizz about the Solar System, too. As far as we know, the Earth is the only place in the Solar System where anything lives.

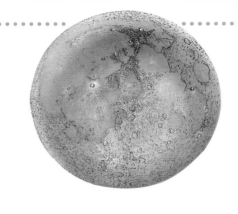

△ The Earth has one moon. It is nearly 400,000 kilometres from Earth (about 240,000 miles). Its diameter is only a quarter of the Earth's.

 Never look straight at the Sun, either with binoculars or just with your eyes.

◁ Try looking at the Moon through a pair of binoculars. Can you see the craters on the surface?

The Solar System is enormous. If the Sun was only the size of a football, the Earth would be the size of a pin head, 25 metres away. Pluto would be more than one kilometre from the Sun.

▽ Mercury, Venus, Earth and Mars are small, rocky planets. Mercury is nearest the Sun.

▷ Jupiter and Saturn are huge. They are made of gas and liquid. Jupiter is the biggest of all the planets. The others could all fit inside it easily.

Jupiter

Mercury

Venus

Earth

Mars

▽ This is the spacecraft Voyager 2. It is a space probe. It was sent from Earth in 1977 to explore outer space. It reached Neptune in 1989. Scientists have learned a lot about planets from Voyager 2 and other spacecraft like it.

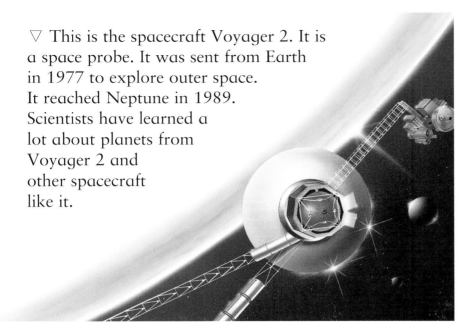

▷ If you are lucky, you might see streaks of light, called shooting stars or meteors, in the night sky. They are made by rocks called meteoroids hurtling into the Earth's atmosphere and burning up.

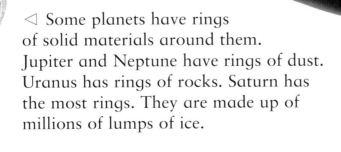

Saturn

◁ Some planets have rings of solid materials around them. Jupiter and Neptune have rings of dust. Uranus has rings of rocks. Saturn has the most rings. They are made up of millions of lumps of ice.

▽ Pluto is the furthest planet from the Sun. It is smaller than the Earth's moon.

Uranus

Neptune

• **Pluto**

Find out more
Earth
Satellites
Universe

Solids

A solid is one of the three states of matter. The others are liquids and gases. A solid has a fixed shape. It does not flow around like a liquid or a gas. This is because the atoms are joined firmly together, and can hardly move about at all.

△ In some solids, the atoms are arranged in neat rows. This sort of solid is called a crystal.

◁ **1** This is how to make sugar crystals grow. Stir some sugar into warm water until no more will dissolve.

▷ **2** Pour the liquid into a saucer and leave it in a warm place, so that the water evaporates. Can you see the crystals beginning to form?

△ These objects are made from solids that are not crystals. Although their atoms are not in neat rows, they still cannot move about.

▽ Some solids are softer than others. The soft, grey substance in pencils is called graphite. It rubs easily onto the paper when you write.

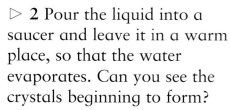

△ Diamond and graphite are both made of carbon, but their atoms are arranged in a different way. Diamond is extremely hard. It is used in jewellery and to make tools for cutting, such as drills.

Find out more
Gases
Materials

266

Sound

Sound is made by vibrations. When you speak, you make vibrations in the air. These vibrations spread out. Anyone whose ears can pick up the vibrations will hear the sound of your voice. Sound can travel through solids and liquids as well as through air and other gases.

Loudness

▽ To see the vibrations that give us sound, cover a plastic pot with a piece of balloon, and secure it with a rubber band. Sprinkle salt on it. Speak near the balloon. The vibrations will make the salt grains jump up and down.

rocket on take off 150–190 decibels

◁ The loudness of a sound depends on the size of the vibrations it makes. Sounds are loud when the vibrations are very big, and soft when they are small. Loudness is measured in units called decibels. The noise of a road drill is over 100 decibels.

motorcycle 70–90 decibels

talking quietly 30–60 decibels

△ This road drill makes a very loud noise. Sounds this loud can damage people's ears. The workers using the drill must cover their ears to protect them.

▽ As sound spreads, the molecules making up the air are squashed together, pulled apart, squashed again, and so on, making sound waves.

leaves rustling 20 decibels

A sound can be high-pitched or low-pitched. The pitch of a sound (how high it is) depends on its frequency (the number of vibrations it makes per second).

▷ Try this experiment to make high- and low-pitched sounds. Pour some water into jars, so the level is different in each. Tap the jars with a pen. Which jar makes the sound with the highest pitch?

▷ Sonar is a way of finding things under water, using sound. A sonar machine on a ship sends "blip" sounds into the water. When these hit an object, they bounce back as echoes. The further away the object is, the longer the echo takes to return to the control ship.

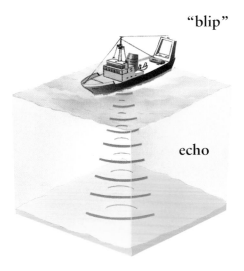

"blip"

echo

Fact box
• A rocket taking off makes a sound a million times louder than a clap of thunder.
• Some animals can hear sounds that are too high- or low-pitched for humans to hear.

◁ Some dolphins make clicking sounds and then listen for their echoes. This helps them to find their way around in murky water. It works in a similar way to sonar. Some kinds of whales communicate with each other using sound. The noises they make can travel hundreds of kilometres across the oceans.

▷ This brass horn looks like a long, coiled tube with a funnel. It makes a sound when the musician blows into the tube and the air inside it vibrates. The funnel spreads the sound out so you can hear it. Do you know any other brass instruments?

△ The cello is a stringed instrument. It makes a sound when the strings vibrate from side to side. This happens when a musician draws a bow across the strings or plucks them. Guitars and violins are also stringed instruments.

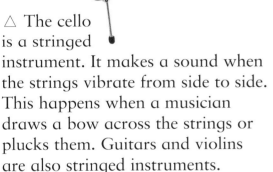

△ This girl is playing a flute. The boy is playing a whistle. Both of these are wind instruments. Like brass instruments, these make a sound when the musician blows into them and the air in the tube vibrates.

◁ This girl is playing an electronic keyboard. Keyboards like these are sometimes called synthesizers. A synthesizer makes sounds through a loudspeaker. Each key makes a note of a different pitch.

Find out more
Energy
Physics
Senses

South America

South America is the fourth largest continent. Down one side runs a long line of mountains called the Andes. The world's largest rainforest grows around the Amazon River. It has hot and cold deserts and large grassy plains. Many of South America's people live in crowded cities and are very poor.

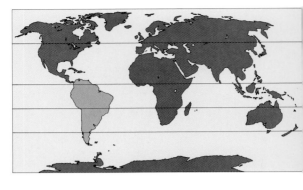

△ South America is shown in purple. It is joined to North America by a thin stretch of land.

▷ The people who live around Lake Titicaca, in the Andes, build their boats and houses out of reeds.

◁ Statues and ruins are all that is left of the ancient cities of South America. This statue is from a city called Tiahuanaco.

▷ Llamas are kept for their meat and wool and are used to carry heavy goods up mountain roads.

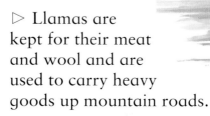

▷ Cowboys, called gauchos, look after enormous herds of cattle on the grassy plains of Argentina. The grasslands are called the pampas.

▽ Angel Falls, in the thick rainforest of Venezuela, is the highest waterfall in the world.

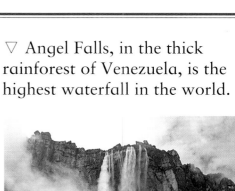

▷ Macaws live in the lush Amazon rainforest. Snakes, monkeys and big cats also live there.

scarlet macaw

◁ Above the city of Rio de Janeiro stands a huge statue of Christ. Rio is the main port of Brazil. Its beautiful bay is surrounded by mountains.

Find out more
Conservation
Grasslands
World

Space exploration

To find out more about the planets and stars, rockets are used to carry people and objects into Space. People who travel into Space are called astronauts. They have to wear special suits in Space to survive. Spacecraft are machines that can travel into Space. One of the best known is the Space Shuttle.

▽ The Space Shuttle can carry up to seven astronauts into Space. Its doors open up in Space to release its cargo of scientific instruments. An astronaut controls a robot arm to move the cargo.

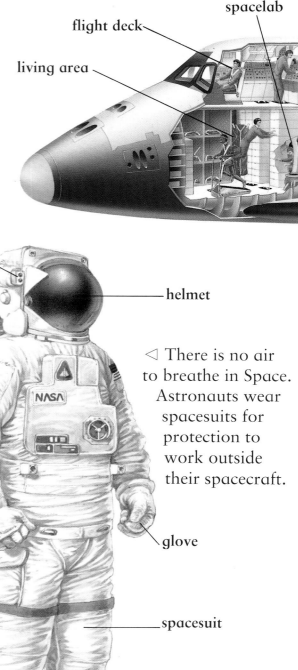

tunnel to spacelab

flight deck

living area

Saturn V

radio

helmet

air supply

◁ The biggest rocket ever built was called the Saturn V. It carried the first astronauts to the Moon in 1969.

◁ There is no air to breathe in Space. Astronauts wear spacesuits for protection to work outside their spacecraft.

NASA

glove

spacesuit

boot

Space Shuttle

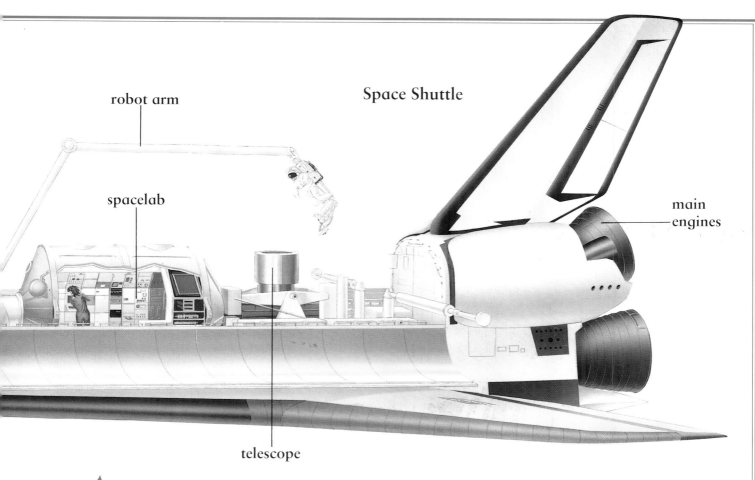

robot arm

spacelab

main engines

telescope

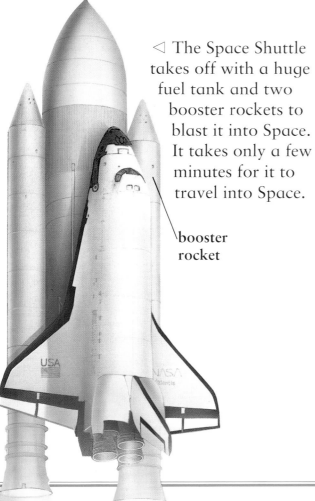

◁ The Space Shuttle takes off with a huge fuel tank and two booster rockets to blast it into Space. It takes only a few minutes for it to travel into Space.

booster rocket

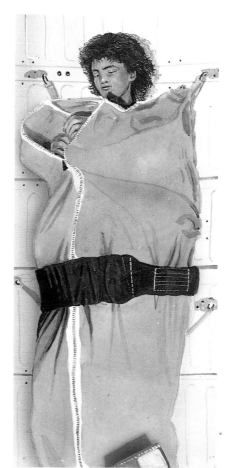

◁ In Space nothing has any weight. Astronauts have to move around carefully. They are strapped into their sleeping bags to stop them floating around.

Satellites and probes

Rockets also carry satellites and probes into Space. These machines send back information to Earth.

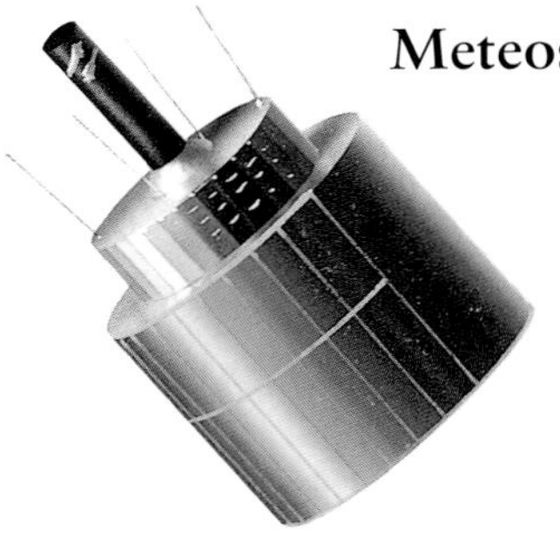

Meteosat

▷ The giant Hubble Space Telescope sends back pictures of stars and galaxies to astronomers on Earth.

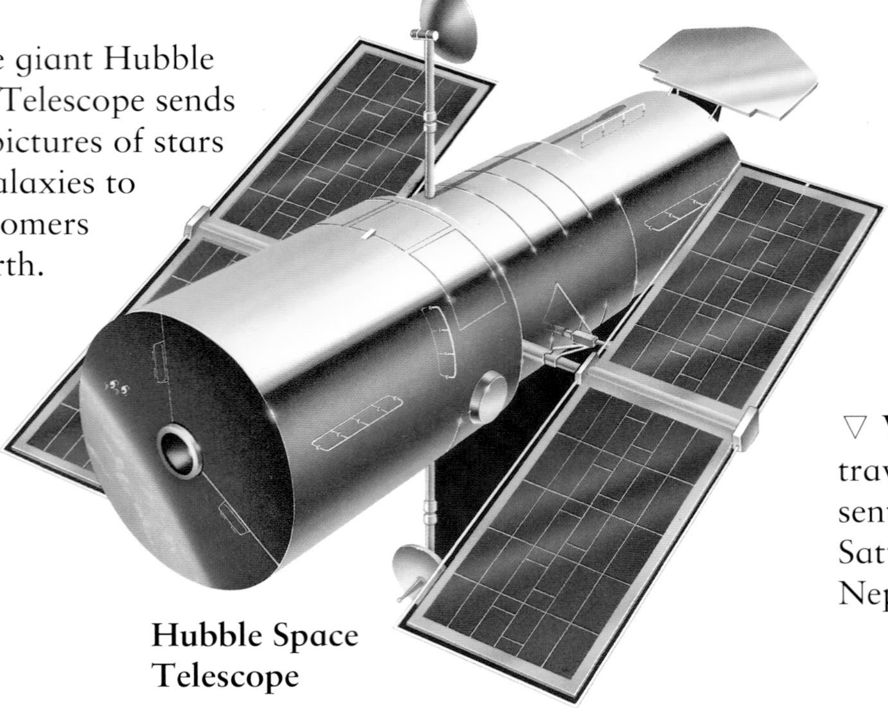

Hubble Space Telescope

△ Meteosat watches weather patterns. It sends information to computers on Earth.

▽ Voyager 2 was a probe that travelled out to the planets. It sent back pictures of Jupiter, Saturn, Uranus and Neptune.

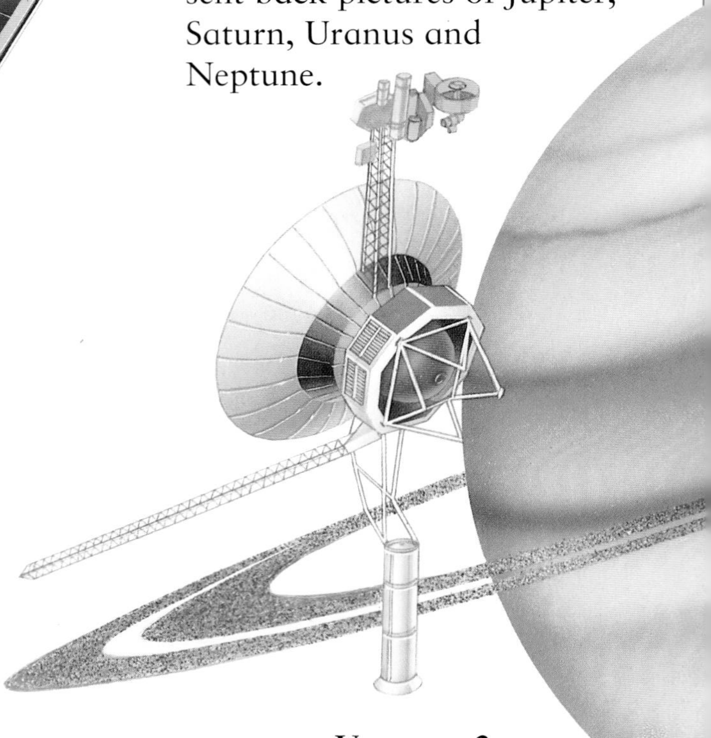

Voyager 2

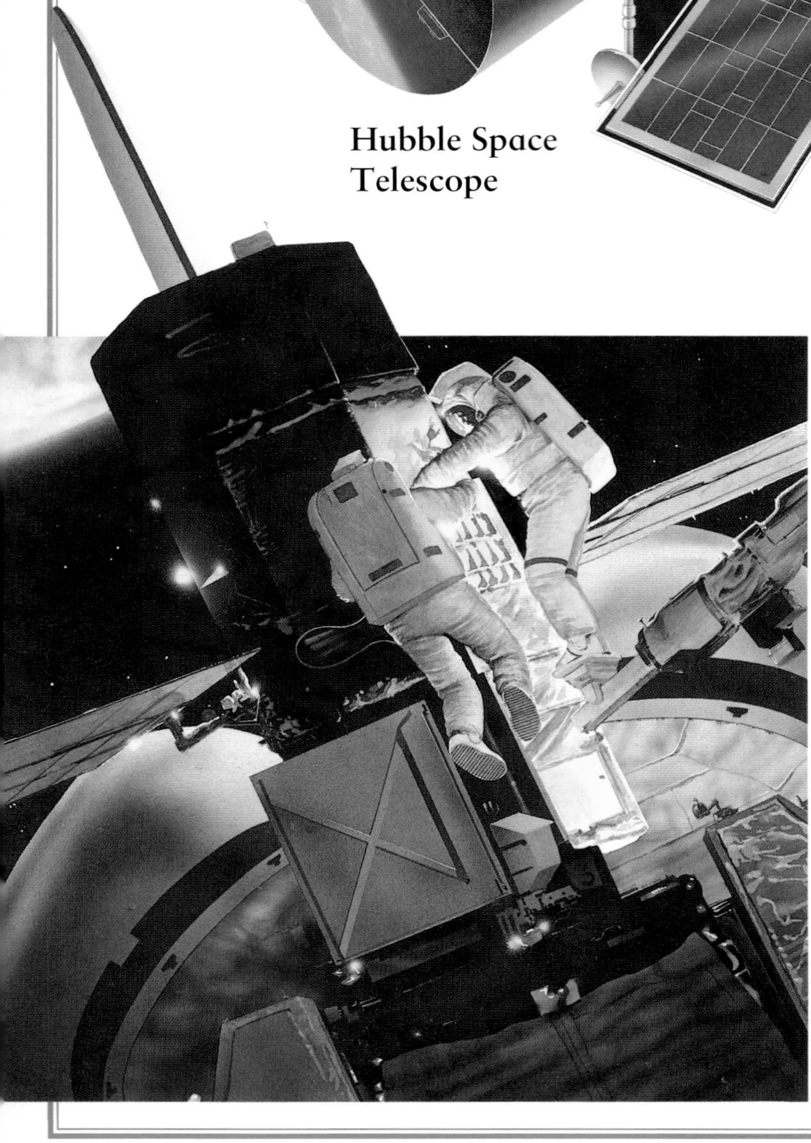

◁ These astronauts are mending a broken satellite. The satellite has been taken into the Space Shuttle's repair bay.

Find out more
Inventions
Moon
Universe

Spider

Spiders belong to the class of animals called arachnids. They feed mainly on insects. Most spiders have large, hairy, round abdomens (rear body parts) and eight legs. All spiders make silk and many spin webs.

◁ The female black widow spider is one of the few spiders with venom (poison) harmful to humans. Most people bitten by it do recover fully.

Fact box

• The goliath bird-eating spider is the biggest spider in the world. It is large enough to cover a dinner plate.
• Tropical orb-web spiders build some of the largest webs, at nearly two metres across.

△ Camel spiders live in deserts in Africa and Asia. They do not spin webs, but pounce on their prey and crush them in their strong jaws. They feed on scorpions, birds and small lizards.

▷ Many spiders spin webs of sticky silk to catch their prey. Silk is very strong and it is also stretchy. Here a garden spider wraps a fly in its silk, then stuns it with venom from its fangs.

◁ Spiders live in many places, from hot deserts to cold areas, and from mountains to lakes. Some spiders that live near water eat small fish.

Find out more
Fly
Insect
Scorpion

Sports

People play sports for many reasons. It may be their job or they may do it just for fun. Sport helps them to stay fit and healthy. Some sports are played by one person. Others are played by two or more people. In many sports two teams compete with each other. Some sports, like horse racing, involve animals as well as people.

△ Football is played all over the world. In some countries it is called soccer. Footballers need great skill to control the ball with their feet.

▷ Baseball is one of the favourite team sports in America. This boy is called the pitcher.

◁ Gymnasts must learn from a young age how to perform difficult exercises on the floor and on special pieces of equipment, like this one, called the bar.

◁ In Mongolia, boys and girls as young as five dress up to take part in horse races.

▷ Ice-hockey is Canada's most popular sport. It is a fast and tough game. Helmets and pads are worn for protection.

△ Swimmers train hard to swim fast. They learn different strokes, called breaststroke, backstroke, front crawl and butterfly.

▽ When two people play tennis against each other it is called singles. When four play it is called doubles.

▷ The Olympic Games are held every four years. Countries send their best athletes to compete.

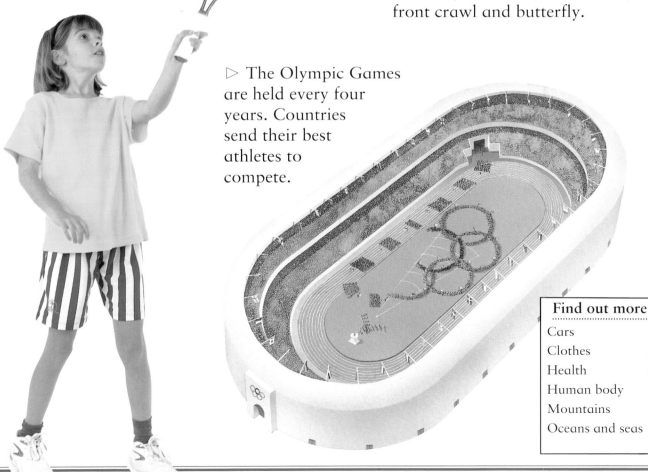

Find out more

Cars
Clothes
Health
Human body
Mountains
Oceans and seas

Squirrel

Most squirrels have big, bushy tails and live in trees. They are active during the day, running from branch to branch in search of nuts, fruit and seeds.

▷ The red squirrel, like the one seen here, is smaller than its grey cousin. In Britain, red squirrels are being forced from their woodland homes by the more aggressive grey squirrels, which were imported from North America about 100 years ago.

▽ The prairie dog is a burrowing squirrel that lives on North American grasslands. Their large underground burrows, called towns, contain up to 1,000 prairie dogs.

◁ Squirrels love seeds like acorns, which they gnaw with their sharp front teeth. In autumn, they sometimes bury a supply in the ground to last them through the winter.

Find out more
Habitat
Mammal
Mouse
Rat
Reproduction

Starfish

Starfish are found on seabeds worldwide, especially in the warm waters of the Indian and Pacific Oceans. Though starfish are star shaped, they are not fish. They have no head and no brain; all they have is five or more arms, a central body and a mouth.

1

2

3

4

◁ A starfish has hundreds of strong suckers called tube feet. If it is turned upside down it uses these tube feet to turn over again. **1** It curls the tips of its arms around to grip the rocks with its suckers. **2** When it has a hold, it pulls itself over slowly. **3,4** It flops down the right way up, and moves off.

△ There are 1,500 species of starfish in the world's oceans. Many are brightly coloured.

▷ Some kinds of starfish have lots of legs, like this sunstar. If a starfish loses a leg, it can easily grow another.

▽ Starfish eat shellfish. To eat a mussel, the starfish opens the shell with its powerful suckers, then pushes its stomach out of its mouth and onto the body of the shellfish.

Fact box

• The crown-of-thorns starfish feeds on coral, and this can badly damage the reef.
• Starfish sense changes in light with the light-sensitive spots on the ends of their arms.
• Some starfish lay up to a million eggs in a year.

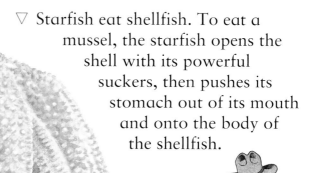

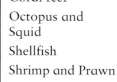

Find out more
Coral reef
Octopus and Squid
Shellfish
Shrimp and Prawn

Stories

Stories tell you about events. Some stories are about real things, others are made up. Long ago, people told each other stories about their gods or about real people who had done amazing things. Now we read stories in books, comics or watch them in films and on television.

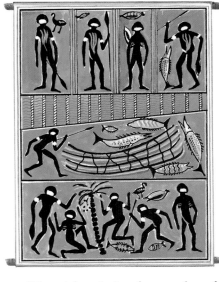

△ The Aboriginal people of Australia paint stories to tell how the land was made.

▽ Use your imagination to write and illustrate your own story. Make it a scary, funny or magical story. Draw pictures of the characters.

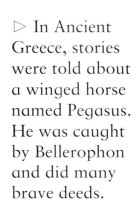

▷ In Ancient Greece, stories were told about a winged horse named Pegasus. He was caught by Bellerophon and did many brave deeds.

◁ In Ghana, in Africa, people tell stories about a spider called Anansi who likes to play tricks.

▷ Comic strips tell stories with pictures. The words people say are written in speech bubbles.

▷ Jack and the Beanstalk is a folk tale. Jack climbs a huge beanstalk to steal a magic hen from a wicked and cruel giant.

◁ The story of the Wizard of Oz was made into a famous film. Dorothy helps a scarecrow, a lion and a tin man.

Find out more

Africa

Art and artists

Books

Dance

Drama

Sun

The Sun is a star. It is a dazzling ball of burning gases. The Sun is the nearest, most important star to the Earth. It gives us light and warmth. Earth is just the right distance from the Sun. If Earth was closer to the Sun it would burn up. If it was farther away it would be freezing cold.

△ During an eclipse the Moon hides the Sun. This is the only time we see clouds of white gas, called the corona, that surround the Sun.

Never look straight at the Sun. It will damage your eyes.

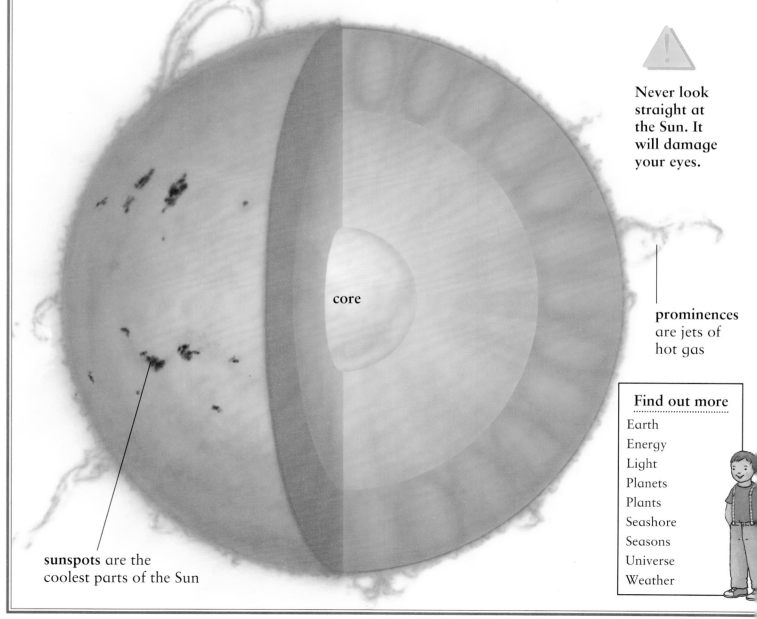

core

prominences are jets of hot gas

sunspots are the coolest parts of the Sun

Find out more

Earth
Energy
Light
Planets
Plants
Seashore
Seasons
Universe
Weather

Swan

The swan is one of the world's largest water birds, with a wingspan of up to three metres. It has webbed feet for swimming and a wide beak for eating underwater plants. Swans guard their eggs closely and will attack humans if they feel threatened.

trumpeter swan

△ Swans in the Northern Hemisphere are white. Most are named after their calls, such as the trumpeter, whistling and whooper swans. The whistling swan migrates from the Canadian Arctic to spend the winter in the southern United States.

▽ Southern swans include the Australian black swan and the South American black-necked swan.

Australian black swan

Fact box

• Swans live for 20 years or more.
• Swans swallow stones to help their digestion. But many have accidentally eaten anglers' lead weights and been poisoned by them.
• Swans build a big nest that can float on the water.

△ Swans mate when they are five years old and the pairs remain loyal for life. Young swans, called cygnets, have fluffy grey feathers and short necks that make them look more like scruffy ducks. Their long necks and white plumage grow when they are a year old.

Find out more
Bird
Duck and Goose
Migration
Pelican

Technology

Technology means designing and using tools and machines. It also means the tools and machines themselves. Computers, cars, tin openers and cameras are all examples of technology. We use technology at home, at school and when we travel from place to place. At work, technology helps people do their jobs more quickly and easily. Some technology is very complicated. Some is very simple.

△ Computer technology can help people with disabilities. For example, people who cannot use their hands can talk into a computer and it will write what they say.

△ Above are some of the different kinds of technology that people have in their homes. There is a television, a radio, a telephone, a computer and a video. What kinds of technology do you have in your home?

▷ Building technology is used to design houses, tunnels, dams and bridges. Choosing the right materials and making the design strong and safe are important parts of building technology. This is the Bay Bridge in San Francisco in America.

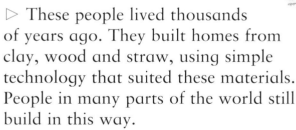

◁ Modern technology began towards the end of the 1700s. This early steam engine, the *Adler*, opened the first German public railway in 1835. The first engines reached speeds of 50 to 60 kilometres per hour, which people thought was amazingly fast.

▷ These people lived thousands of years ago. They built homes from clay, wood and straw, using simple technology that suited these materials. People in many parts of the world still build in this way.

◁ This machine is called a shaduf. It is used in Egypt and other parts of the Middle East to take water from rivers to nearby fields. People have been using shadufs for over 3,000 years. The design has not changed because it works well and is easy to look after.

Find out more
Calculator
Computers
Engines
Inventions and Discoveries
Machines

Telephones

What happens if you want to speak to someone at the other end of your street, or in a different town or country? You probably use a telephone. Your telephone is linked to other telephones through the telephone network. Every telephone has its own number. When you dial the number of your friend's telephone, this links your telephone through the network to your friend's telephone.

△ Early telephones had no buttons or dials. You asked the telephone operator to connect you to the number you wanted.

1

△ **1** Make a simple telephone. You need two empty yoghurt pots and some string. Make a small hole in the base of each pot. Ask an adult to help you.

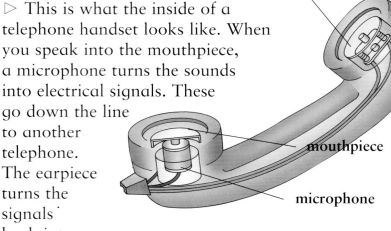

▷ This is what the inside of a telephone handset looks like. When you speak into the mouthpiece, a microphone turns the sounds into electrical signals. These go down the line to another telephone. The earpiece turns the signals back into sound.

earpiece

mouthpiece

microphone

Fact box

• The telephone was invented in America in 1876 by Alexander Graham Bell, a Scottish engineer and teacher.

▷ **2** Push one end of the string into one of the holes. Tie a knot to stop it slipping out. Do the same thing with the other yoghurt pot. Make sure the knots are tight.

2

one person holds a pot over their ear

▷ A telephone is linked to an exchange. Exchanges are connected to each other, by cables, radio and sometimes by satellite links. All these things make up the telephone network.

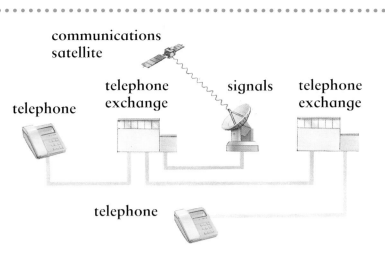

communications
satellite

telephone
exchange

signals

telephone
exchange

telephone

telephone

△ The telephones we use at home are linked to the local exchange by wires. Signals go along these as pulses of electricity. Some telephone cables are made of thin glass fibres called optical fibres. Signals travel along these as flashes of light.

△ A fax machine plugs into a telephone line, just like an ordinary telephone. It has a scanner that turns words and pictures into electrical signals. The fax sends these to another fax machine.

△ The other fax machine turns the signals back into words and pictures. It prints them onto paper.

the other person
talks into a pot

3

the string
must be
pulled tight

◁ 3 Vibrations made by your voice travel along the string. They make the other pot vibrate. Your friend hears these vibrations as your voice.

Find out more
Electricity
Inventions and
Discoveries
Satellites
Sound

Television

What sort of television programmes do you like best? To make a televison programme, a camera has to take pictures. These go from the camera to a television station, and on to a transmitter. This sends them to your television set, along wires or on radio waves. Satellite television programmes travel on microwaves.

△ The pictures on these screens are from security cameras. A guard watches for intruders. A system like this is called closed circuit television.

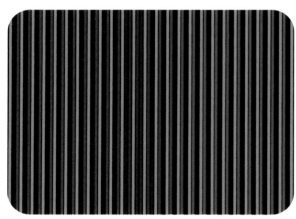

△ This is a magnified close-up of a television screen. You can see bands of red, green and blue. All television pictures are made up of just these three colours.

△ This camera is recording a sporting event. The camera operator sees the picture the camera is taking on a small television screen.

screen

speaker

◁ A television set turns signals from the television station into the pictures you see on the screen. It plays sound through the loudspeakers.

Find out more
Colour
Electricity
Light
Microwaves
Radio
Video

Tiger

Tigers are the biggest of all cats. They live in the grasslands and forests of Asia, where their striped coat gives them good camouflage when they hunt.

△ Female tigers give birth to between one and three cubs. The cubs stay with their mother for over a year.

△ A tiger slowly stalks its prey, a deer, through the long grass. When it is close enough, it makes a sudden dash, leaps onto the deer's back and knocks it down. A quick bite to the neck kills the deer.

◁ Tigers are hunted for their beautiful coats, and for their bones and body parts, which are used in traditional Chinese medicine. Because of this, tigers are nearly extinct.

Find out more

Cat (wild)
Cheetah
Lion

Time

We use clocks and watches to measure time exactly in hours, minutes and seconds. Before clocks and watches were invented people measured time roughly in days, nights and seasons. Later people used candle clocks and shadow clocks, which were not as accurate as the clocks we have today.

candle clock

◁ Candle clocks were marked in sections. The candle burned away one section every hour. People could tell the time by the number of sections left.

video machine

△ This video recorder has a digital clock. It uses the clock to start a recording at the right time.

alarm clock

△ An alarm clock can be set to wake you up in time for something. Many children need alarm clocks to wake them up in time for school.

stopwatch

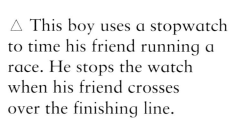

△ This boy uses a stopwatch to time his friend running a race. He stops the watch when his friend crosses over the finishing line.

Find out more
Earth
Machines
Moon
Seasons
Year

Trains

All over the world, trains pull heavy loads along rails. The rails make it easier for the wheels to turn. The first trains used steam engines to drive the wheels. Now, most trains run on electricity or diesel fuel. Trains carry people and goods for long distances, at high speeds.

steam train

△ Steam trains were invented 200 years ago. They used coal or wood to make steam to drive the wheels.

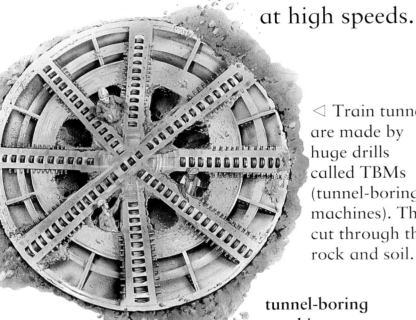

◁ Train tunnels are made by huge drills called TBMs (tunnel-boring machines). They cut through the rock and soil.

tunnel-boring machine

△ Many overcrowded cities have underground trains. The trains run on electrified rails and carry people through tunnels under the city.

coal wagon   flatcar   diesel engine

◁ Trains that carry goods are called freight trains. Some can pull over 100 wagons.

◁ The Japanese Bullet train can travel as fast as 300 km per hour.

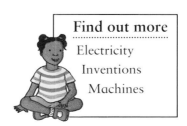

Find out more

Electricity
Inventions
Machines

291

Trees

Trees are plants. They are the largest living things on Earth. Many of them live for hundreds of years.

Trees give food and shelter to birds, insects and many other animals. Mushrooms and other fungi grow on their roots and on dead tree stumps.

△ Each year, a layer of wood grows inside the trunk of a tree and makes a ring. You can tell how old a tree was by counting the number of rings in the trunk.

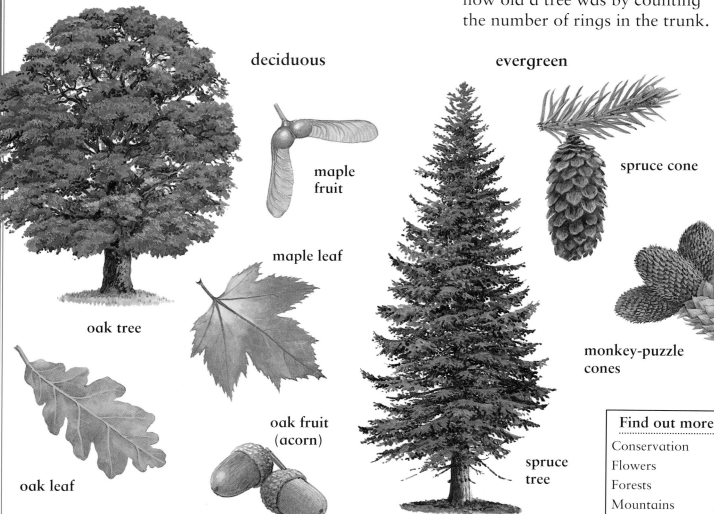

deciduous

maple fruit

maple leaf

oak tree

oak leaf

oak fruit (acorn)

evergreen

spruce cone

monkey-puzzle cones

spruce tree

△ Deciduous trees start to lose their leaves in autumn and have no leaves in winter. They grow new leaves in the spring.

△ Evergreen trees keep their leaves all year. Many have spiky, needle-like leaves that are not harmed by the cold.

Find out more
Conservation
Flowers
Forests
Mountains
Plants
Prehistoric life
Seasons

Trucks

Trucks carry all sorts of things in huge containers, called trailers. Many travel long distances from one country to another. Others travel much shorter distances. Some bring food and goods to shops. Others take materials to and from factories. Trucks are also called lorries.

△ This truck is called a road train. Road trains can pull three huge trailers. They are used in Australia.

△ The crane on the back of a logging truck is used to lift logs onto the trailer. This truck is used in places with large forests.

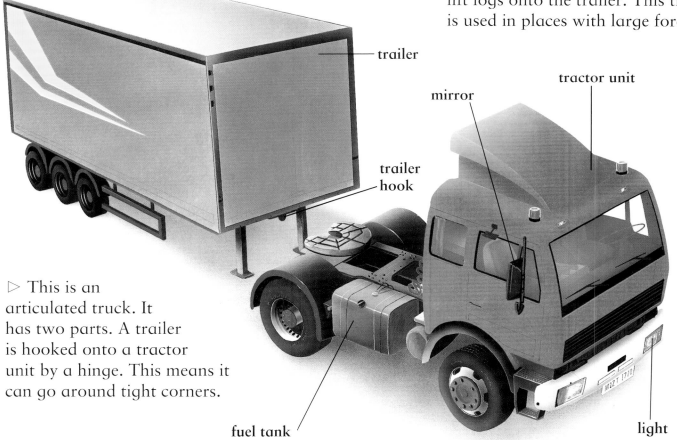

trailer

trailer hook

mirror

tractor unit

fuel tank

light

▷ This is an articulated truck. It has two parts. A trailer is hooked onto a tractor unit by a hinge. This means it can go around tight corners.

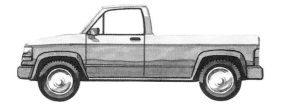

◁ Small pick-up trucks, like this one, have open backs. They are used all over the world.

Find out more
Conservation
Machines
Roads

Turtle and Tortoise

Turtles and tortoises are reptiles that live in warm climates. Turtles are found in water; tortoises are slow land animals. The soft bodies of both animals are protected by a heavy shell.

Fact box
• The marine green turtle can swim a distance of 480km in only ten days.
• Terrapin is the name given to some freshwater turtles.
• The huge marine leatherback turtle can be 2.7m in length.

△ Many turtles spend nearly all their lives in the sea. Their legs are shaped like paddles, which helps them to swim. Only females ever come onto land. They do this to lay eggs – on the same beach as they were born.

◁ Tortoises are found in Africa, Asia, Europe, and North and South America. They grow slowly and can live to be over 150 years old.

◁ **1** The female turtle crawls out of the sea to lay her eggs. **2** She buries them in a hole, then returns to the water. The sun's heat keeps them warm until they are ready to hatch.

▷ **3** Left on their own, the tiny babies must break free of their eggs and dig their way out of the hole. **4** They must hurry to the sea before they are eaten by other animals.

Find out more
Chameleon
Lizard
Reptile
Reproduction

Universe

The Earth, the Sun, the Moon and all the planets and stars are all part of the Universe. The Earth is just one planet that circles around our Sun. The Sun and all the stars you can see in the sky at night make up our galaxy, called the Milky Way. The Milky Way is a tiny part of the Universe. Everything, even light, energy, animals and plants, is part of the Universe. It is very hard to imagine how big the Universe really is.

△ Even when you look through a telescope you can only see a tiny part of the Universe.

◁ This picture is of huge groups of stars, called galaxies. It was taken in space by the Hubble Space Telescope.

Hubble Space Telescope

The life of a star

New stars are being made all the time. They shine for a very long time and then they die. A red giant is a huge, old star.

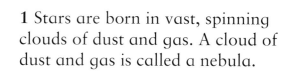

Little Bear

Southern Cross

△ Long ago, people gave names to patterns of stars in the sky. These are called constellations. The Little Bear can be seen by people living in northern parts of the world. The Southern Cross can be seen by people living in the south.

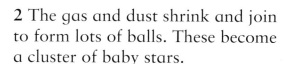

1 Stars are born in vast, spinning clouds of dust and gas. A cloud of dust and gas is called a nebula.

2 The gas and dust shrink and join to form lots of balls. These become a cluster of baby stars.

3 As a star gets hotter it begins to shine. Most stars, like our Sun, shine steadily nearly all their lives.

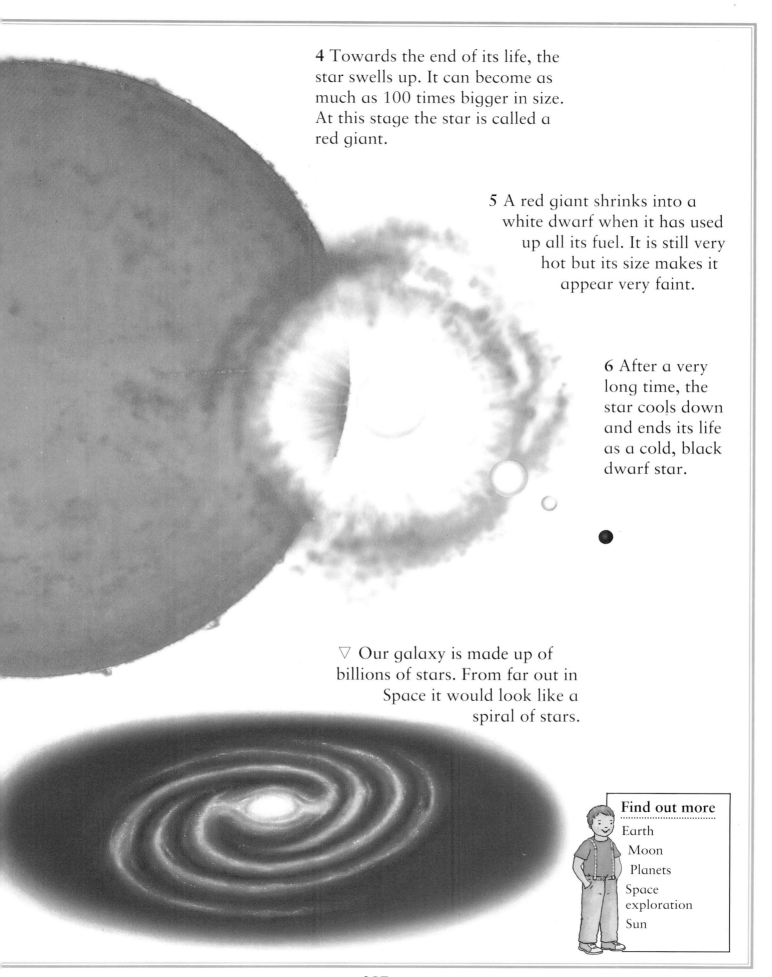

4 Towards the end of its life, the star swells up. It can become as much as 100 times bigger in size. At this stage the star is called a red giant.

5 A red giant shrinks into a white dwarf when it has used up all its fuel. It is still very hot but its size makes it appear very faint.

6 After a very long time, the star cools down and ends its life as a cold, black dwarf star.

▽ Our galaxy is made up of billions of stars. From far out in Space it would look like a spiral of stars.

Find out more
Earth
Moon
Planets
Space exploration
Sun

Video

Video is a way of recording moving pictures. The recording is done on video tape. This is like the tape used in a music cassette. With a video camera, you can record your own moving pictures and play them later on your television, using a video machine.

▽ A camcorder is a video camera and recorder all in one. You look through the viewfinder to see what you are recording.

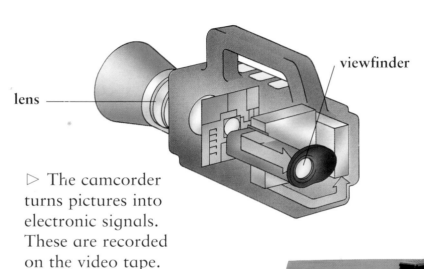

lens

viewfinder

▷ The camcorder turns pictures into electronic signals. These are recorded on the video tape.

◁ A video machine is used to record television programmes for watching later. It can also play pre-recorded video tapes, such as films and cartoons.

◁ The word video also describes moving pictures made by a computer. That's why computer games are sometimes called video games.

Find out more
Camera
Electricity
Recording
Television

Volcano

Under the Earth's hard crust lies hot, molten rock called magma. Sometimes pressure builds up under the Earth and pushes the magma up through cracks in the crust. This is how a volcano erupts. When it reaches the surface, the magma is known as lava. Some volcanoes erupt with a bang and shoot gas, dust and lava into the air.

△ These huge fountains of hot water and steam are called geysers. They are often found near volcanoes. Water is heated by the hot rocks under the ground and gushes to the surface through cracks in the Earth's crust.

△ 1 Make a model volcano. Put about two teaspoons of bicarbonate of soda into a spice jar. Build a clay model of a volcano around the jar.

△ 2 Pour 100 ml of vinegar into the jar and watch your volcano erupt. To make coloured lava, add food colouring to the vinegar.

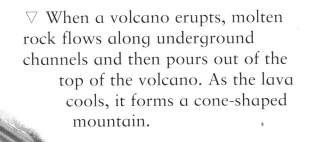

▽ When a volcano erupts, molten rock flows along underground channels and then pours out of the top of the volcano. As the lava cools, it forms a cone-shaped mountain.

△ The hole at the top of a volcano is called the crater. In some volcanoes, smoke rises from the crater all the time.

Find out more
Earth
Energy
Fuels
Melting and
Boiling

Vulture

Vultures are large, strange-looking birds with wide wingspans. They are found worldwide – on mountains and plains, and in forests. They feed on rotting meat.

◁ Many species of vulture, like the king vulture (left), have no head or neck feathers. This keeps them clean when feeding. The king vulture's brightly coloured skin flaps are used in mating displays.

△ Many vulture species have incredible eyesight. They fly high in the air, looking for predators' kills.

▽ Vultures do a vital job because they clean up the carcasses left behind by predators. Once they spot a carcass, they glide down to feed. Some vultures have adapted to living in towns, and scavenge on rubbish dumps.

△ Vultures, like this white-backed vulture, often sit in the trees around a lion or hyena kill, waiting until the larger animals have had their fill.

Eurasian griffin

Ruppell's griffin

African white-backed vulture

lappet-faced vulture

Find out more
Bird
Eagle
Owl

Water

All life on Earth needs water. Without it everything would die. Water covers nearly three-quarters of the world. There is salty water in the oceans and seas, and fresh water in lakes, rivers and ponds. Frozen water, or ice, usually covers the oceans around Antarctica and in the Arctic. All these watery places are home to many different plants and animals.

pond skater

△ A pond skater can walk on water because of a force called surface tension. This force makes a thin stretchy layer on the water.

▷ When water is a liquid it flows and spreads. It fills the container that it is poured into and it has a flat surface.

water

▷ If water becomes very cold it freezes and turns into solid ice. When ice melts it turns back into water.

ice

▽ When water is very hot it boils. Tiny bubbles rise up, burst and release steam.

steam

▽ Steam cools when it hits something cold and turns into water droplets. This change is called condensation.

condensation

301

How we use water
▷ **1** Water falls as rain and runs into streams and rivers. It is collected and stored in big lakes called reservoirs.

▷ **2** The water is cleaned.

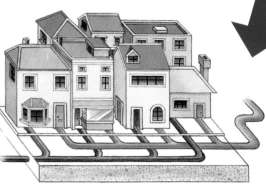

▽ **3** Water is pumped into houses in undergrond pipes.

△ **5** The water is cleaned before it flows back into a river or the sea.

△ **4** After it has been used, the water goes down into big pipes called sewers.

▽ Plants need water. Their roots soak up water from the soil. The water travels up the stems to the leaves where it helps to make food.

Fact box

• You lose water from your body when you sweat, breathe and go to the toilet.

• You need to drink about one litre of water a day to stay healthy.

• You could not live for more than three days without water.

◁ More than two-thirds of your body is made of water.

◁ In the dry grasslands of Africa, groups of animals gather at the waterhole. They watch out for hungry lions as they take a long drink.

▽ This mangrove swamp is a wet area of land near the sea. Mangrove trees usually have long, strong roots to anchor them in the mud.

◁ A salmon swims from the sea to lay its eggs in the stream where it was born. Some bears wait near waterfalls to catch salmon.

▽ Many different plants grow in and around ponds. They provide food, shelter and nesting places for all sorts of birds, insects and other water creatures.

Find out more

Amphibians
Animals
Caves
Energy
Oceans and seas
Fish
Plants
Science
Seashore
Weather
World

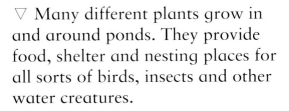

Weather

The weather changes all the time. One day the sky may be clear and sunny, the next it may be cloudy and rainy. Three things cause the weather: air, Sun and water. Air is always on the move and makes the wind. The Sun gives warmth, and the water makes clouds, rain, snow and hail.

▽ This picture shows how the Earth uses its water over and over again. It is called the **water cycle**.

1 Every day, the Sun's heat turns water from seas and lakes into an invisible gas called water vapour.

2 As the air rises, it cools down and the water vapour turns into tiny drops of water or ice crystals.

3 Lots of drops of water join together to make clouds. The wind blows the clouds over the land.

4 Water in the clouds falls as rain, hail, sleet or snow.

5 Rivers carry the water back to the sea.

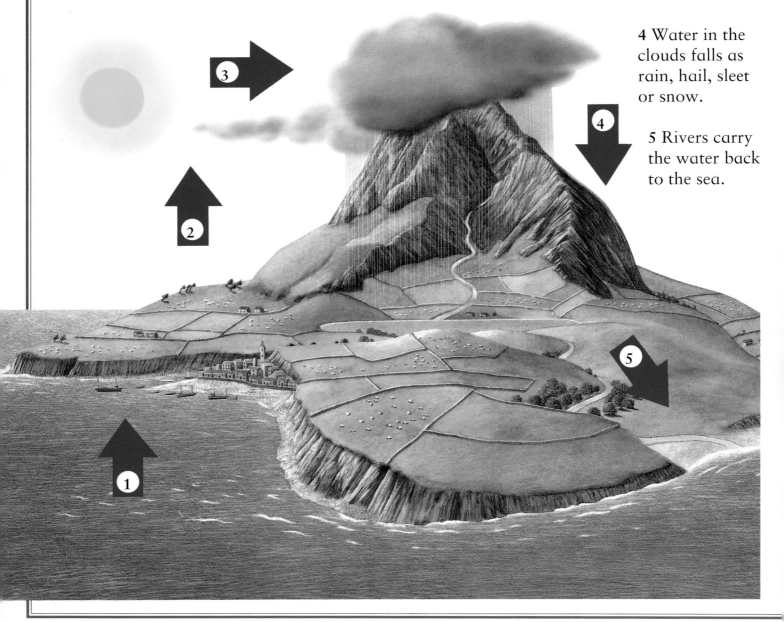

cirrus

stratus

cumulus

cumulonimbus

◁ There are different kinds of cloud. Fluffy clouds are called cumulus. Flat clouds are called stratus. Huge cumulonimbus clouds bring storms. Cirrus clouds are high up and wispy.

▷ Snowflakes are water drops that have frozen into ice crystals. No two snowflakes are ever the same.

▽ In very cold places, ice and snow often cover the land for most of the year.

△ Fog and mist are really clouds floating close to the ground. On roads, thick fog makes it difficult for drivers to see where they are going.

△ Thunderstorms start in big black thunderclouds that gather in the sky.

△ Electricity builds up inside the clouds. This causes big sparks of lightning.

△ When lightning flashes, it heats the air and makes a noise. This is thunder.

◁ A tornado is a spinning funnel of wind that speeds across the ground. As it spins, it sucks up rocks, trees and houses in its path.

△ Hailstones are frozen drops of rain. As they blow about inside a cloud, layers of ice form around them until they are heavy enough to fall.

thermometer

▷ A thermometer is an instrument used to measure the temperature of the air. This shows how hot or how cold it is.

△ A barometer is an instrument used to measure the pressure of the air. If the air pressure changes, it usually means that there will be a change in the weather too.

wind vane

△ A wind vane shows which direction the wind is blowing in. Winds that blow from the west are called westerlies. Winds that blow from the north are called northerlies.

◁ A rain gauge is used to measure rainfall. The rain falls through a funnel into a container. A scale shows how much rain has fallen.

rain gauge

Find out more
Air
Clothes
Earth
Energy
Light
Seasons
Space
exploration
Sun
Water

World

Most of the world is covered by the sea. Only a third is covered by land. There are seven large areas of land, called continents. People have divided most of them into countries. Each country has its own name, its own money and its own flag. There are about 190 countries in the world. Many different peoples live in each one.

▽ On globes and maps a made-up line, called the Equator, divides the world in half. Countries nearest the Equator are the hottest.

globe

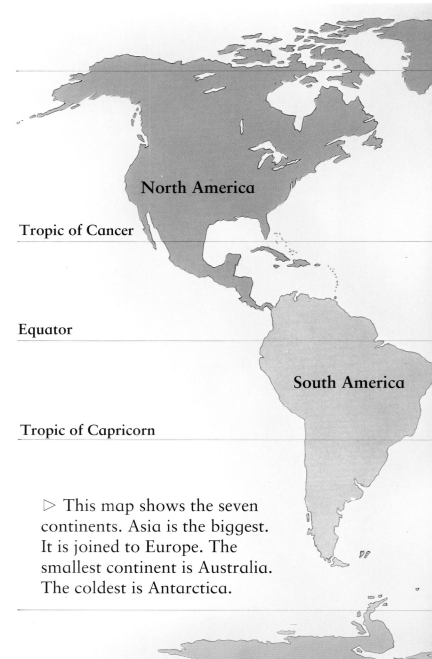

North America

Tropic of Cancer

Equator

South America

Tropic of Capricorn

▷ This map shows the seven continents. Asia is the biggest. It is joined to Europe. The smallest continent is Australia. The coldest is Antarctica.

▷ The world is round. To draw a flat map of it, mapmakers sometimes split its surface into several pieces as if peeling an orange.

Equator

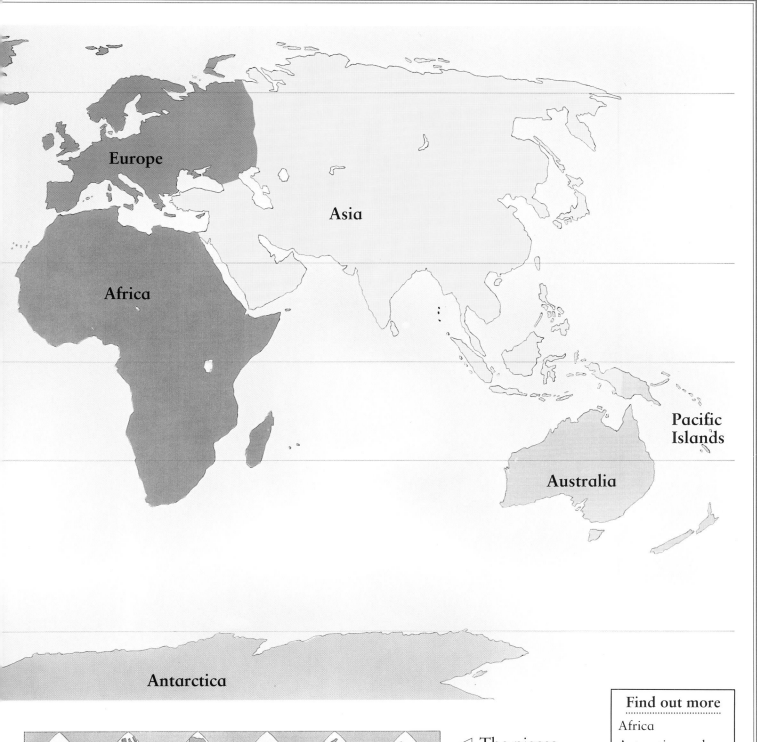

Europe

Asia

Africa

Pacific
Islands

Australia

Antarctica

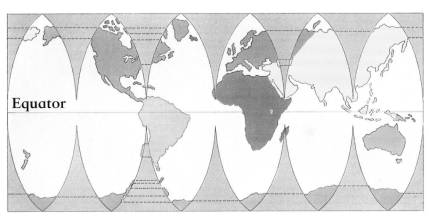

Equator

◁ The pieces
are laid flat
like this. But
this shows that
no flat map
can show the
curved surface
of the world
properly.

X-rays

X-rays are waves, rather like microwaves and light waves. They can pass right through flesh, but not through bones. X-ray photographs are used in hospitals, for example, to see if bones are broken. The bones show up light on a dark background.

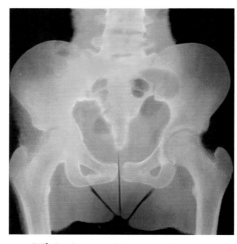

△ This is an X-ray picture of part of a child's back. It was taken to see if any bones were broken.

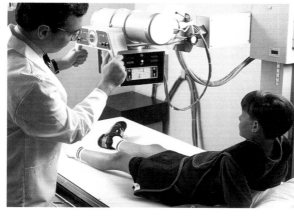

▷ This X-ray machine is being prepared to fire X-rays down through the patient's leg. The X-rays hit a sheet of film on the table beneath.

▽ X-rays are used at airports to check people's baggage for dangerous items. As the bags go through the machine, the screen shows what is inside them.

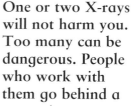

One or two X-rays will not harm you. Too many can be dangerous. People who work with them go behind a protective screen while the X-rays are being taken.

◁ In ancient Egypt, people wrapped dead bodies in cloth to preserve them. These bandaged bodies are called mummies. Modern scientists can use X-rays to look inside the wrappings.

Find out more
Microwaves
Nuclear energy
Radio
Universe

Yak

Yaks are huge, shaggy oxen found on the high plains and mountains of Tibet. Their thick coats keep them warm in the bitter mountain winters. Some are wild, but most are kept as domestic animals.

△ The coats of domestic yaks (above) come in a range of colours from white to black. Wild yaks have long, silky black or brown coats and are bigger than domestic yaks.

▽ The yak was tamed over 2,000 years ago and gives the Tibetan people milk, meat, leather, wool and transport. Yaks are sure-footed in rocky places and can survive in the harshest conditions.

◁Wild yaks are nearly two metres high at the shoulder. The females and young live together in herds . The males prefer to live in smaller groups.

Find out more
Cow and bull
Mammals

Year

A year is a length of time. A year has 365 days. The days are divided into 12 months. Every four years, an extra day is added. This is called a leap year. Throughout the year, celebrations take place all over the world. These may remember important things that have happened during a country's history or celebrate the changing of the seasons.

△ July 4th is Independence Day in the United States. Americans celebrate this day with parades, marching bands, picnics, pageants and fireworks.

▷ Chinese New Year is celebrated between January and February. People dress up and set off noisy firecrackers in the street.

▽ Each year, you probably have a birthday party to celebrate the day you were born. Which day is yours on?

Find out more
Babies
Moon
Seasons

Zebra

Closely related to horses, zebras are grazing mammals that live on the grasslands of Africa, south of the Sahara desert. Their striped coats make it hard for other animals to spot them. Even if they are seen, zebras can run faster than most of their predators.

△ Zebras live in family groups with one stallion (male), several mares (females) and their foals (young). If threatened by a lion, the mares lead the foals to safety, while the stallion kicks out with his powerful back legs.

Fact box

• Zebras are smaller than horses: 2.2m long and 1.3m tall.
• Young females leave the family at two years old. They must then search for a new family to join.
• Males leave the family at four years old.

△ When there is plenty of grass to eat and water to drink, several zebra families may join together to form a large herd. If food becomes scarce, the herd may migrate long distances to find new grasslands, sometimes crossing wide rivers.

△ Zebra stripes are like human fingerprints – no two patterns are the same. Grevy's zebra (above) has much finer stripes than the other species.

Find out more
Antelope
Donkey
Giraffe
Horse

Glossary

A **glossary** is a list of useful words. Some of the words used in this book may be new to you. You can find out more about them here.

ancestor – a person who lived in your family before you.

antennae – a pair of thin, movable feelers on the heads of insects.

atmosphere – the thick blanket of air that surrounds the whole of the Earth.

atom – a tiny particle of matter. Everything around you is made of atoms joined together.

billion – one thousand million (1,000,000,000).

border – the line where one country ends and another country begins.

carnivore – an animal that eats the meat of other animals.

cell – the basic unit of life. All living things are made up of cells.

domestic animal – an animal that is tame and is used to living near people.

echo – when a sound you hear once bounces off a hard surface so that you can hear it again.

electronics – electric circuits that control machines, such as computers, electronic watches and washing machines.

erosion – when soil and rocks are gradually warn away by wind, water, ice or waves.

force – a push or a pull.

germs – tiny bugs that can cause diseases if they get into your body.

herbivore – an animal that eats plants only.

hibernation – when an animal sleeps through the winter.

invertebrate – an animal without a backbone.

microscope – a device that uses lenses to make tiny objects look much bigger.

migration – when an animal moves from one place to another each year.

molecule – a group of atoms joined together. Some molecules have just a few atoms. Other molecules have thousands of atoms.

nocturnal – an animal that sleeps during the day and hunts for food at night.

nucleus – the central part of an atom.

omnivore – an animal that eats both plants and meat.

pollution – waste materials in the environment, such as poisonous gases, chemicals from factories and rubbish.

prehistoric – a very long time ago, before human history was written down.

primary colours – a set of colours that all other colours are made from.

tides – when the level of the sea goes up and down, usually twice a day.

vertebrate – an animal with a backbone.

weight – the pull of gravity on an object. Everything on Earth has weight.

Index

This index helps you find subjects in the book. It is in alphabetical order. The most important entries are in **dark,** or **bold,** type

H

habitat **141**, 171
hail 304, 305
hamster 139
Hanukkah 236
health **142–143**
hearing 129, 254, 255
heart 152, 153
heat 218
heat energy 101, 102, 103, 132
hedgehog **144**
helicopter 116, 121
heron 114
hibernation 38, 144, 170, 240
Himalayas 29, 213
Hindus 79, 236
hippopotamus (hippo) **145**
history **146–149**
horse **150**, 238, 276, 280
hot-air balloon 115, 120
house 48, 270
Hubble Space Telescope 245, 274, 295
human body **151–153**
hummingbird 18, 44, 71, **154**
hyena **155**, 300

I

ice 20–21, 158, 186, 265, 301, 304, 305, 306
India 69, 79, 91, 99, 110, 205, 236, 237
Indian Ocean 171, 206, 249, 279
inertia 196
insect 60, 118, **156–157**, 238
instrument (music) 269
invention **158–159**
invertebrate 16, 19, **60**, 169
iron 176, 187
Islam 237
Italy 49, 106, 123, 218

J

Japan 26, 29, 91, 237
Jesus 235
jet 120–121
Jews 236

J (second column)

job **160**
jumbo jet 120–121
Jupiter 221, 264, 265, 274

K

kangaroo **161**, 178
Kenya 11, 123
killer whale **162**
koala 31, 163
Koran 237
krill 217

L

ladybird 19, 71
laser 73, 233
leafcutter ant 22, 157
lens 166–167, 191
lever 174
light 53, 70, **164–167**, 191
light energy 101, 103
lightning 97, 98, 306
limestone 59
lion **168**, 178–179, 300, 303
liquid 186, 266, 301
lizard **172**, 240, 241, 275
llama **173**, 270
lorry 293
lung 152, 153

M

macaw 93, 214, 271
machine **174–175**
magnet **176–177**
magnetic field 176
maize 10–11, 123
mammal 18, **178–179**, 227
mammoth 128
mangrove swamp 77, 303
map 308–309
Mars 220, 264
marsupial **161**, **163**, 178
material **180–181**
mathematics **182**
Mauritius 74
measurement **183**
Mecca 237
mechanics 218

medicine 143, **184**
Mediterranean 106
meerkat **185**
melting **186**
Mercury 220, 264, 265
metal 181, **187**
meteoroid 195, 265
Mexico 92, 148, 202, 232
microchip 51, 72
microscope 16, 43, 167, 188, 246
microscopic animal **188**
microwave **189**, 288
Middle East 48, 285
migration 25, 45, 92, 154, **190**, 234, 244, 283, 313
milk 76, 111, 122, 238, 311
millipede 60
mime 91
minibeast **60**, 141
mirage 165
mirror **191**
mole 178, **192**
molecule 63, 133
mollusc 60, 257
money **193**
mongoose 69, 185
monkey 18, **33**, 93, **194**, 271
moon **195**, 220, 245, 264, 272, 282, 295
moray eel 95, 208
moth 17, **50**, 108
motion **196–197**
motorbike 42
motte and bailey castle 56
mountain 29, 173, **198**, 202, 270, 299, 311
mouse **199**
movement energy 101, 102, 103, 104, 105, 132
Mozart, Wolfgang Amadeus 201
Muhammad 237
mummy (Egyptian) 310
muscle 102, 151, 153
music **200–201**
Muslims 237
mussel 257, 279

N

nectar 40, 71, 118, 154, 157

Neptune 221, 265, 274
New Zealand 30, 31, 111, 123
newt 15
Niagara Falls 203
night 21, **80**
nitrogen 12, 186
nocturnal animal 36, 58, 80, 231
North America 138, **202–203**, 308
North American animal 229, 232, 261
North Pole 162, 176, 253
Norway 107
nuclear energy **204**
number **205**

O

ocean **206–207**
octopus 19, 207, **208**
oil 104, 130, 132, 259
orang-utan **209**
orbit 195, 220, 245
orchestra 200
ostrich 44, 210
otter **211**
owl 80, **212**
oxygen 12, 64, 152, 153, 222

P

Pacific Islands **30–31**, 149, 309
Pacific Ocean 30, 206, 211, 244, 249, 258, 279
pampas 138, 271
panda **213**
parasite 223
parrot 169, **214**
passenger jet 120–121
passenger ship 259
peacock 44, **215**
Pegasus (flying horse) 280
pelican **216**
penguin 20, 34, 45, **217**, 251
pet **57**, 86, 89, **139**, 150, 194, 199, 214, 219, 228
petrol engine 42, 105
photograph 47, 53, 159
physics **218**
pig **219**, 241
piston 105

planet 94, **220–221**, 295
plankton 188, 207, 250, 256
plant 118, 169, 170, 184, 198, **222–223**, 227, 238, 239, 302
plastic 9, 63, 158, 180, 181
plate (in the Earth's crust) 94
platypus 179, **224**
plays 91, 147
Pluto 221, 264, 265
polar bear 21, 38, **225**
pollen 36, 40, 118, 119, 157, 238
pollination 118
Pollock, Jackson 27
pollution 74, 132
Polynesia 27, 258
pond 15, 39, 90, 303
potential energy 102, 103
power station 132, 204
prairie 138, 202, 278
prawn **260**
prehistoric life **226–227**
printing press 46, 47
pulley 175
pulling 124–125
pupa (chrysalis) 50, 156
pushing 124–125
pyramid 147, 182

R

rabbit 178, **228**
raccoon 203, **229**
radar 189
radio **230**, 284
radioactivity 204
rain 304, 307
rainbow 70
rainforest 10, 66, 126, 141, 171, 202, 214, 262, 270, 271
rat **231**
rattlesnake **232**
ray (fish) 112, 169
ray (light) 164, 165
recording **233**
recycling 181
red blood cell 152, 173
reindeer **234**
religion **235–237**
reproduction **238–239**
reptile 14, 18, 84–85, **240–241**

rhinoceros (rhino) 155, 171, **242**
rice 28, 110, 111, 122
river 145, 203, 302, 304
road **243**
robot 72, 201
rock 59, 94, 103, 299
rocket 105, 245, 268, 272
rodent 139, 199, 231
Russia 79, 106, 128, 251

S

Sahara Desert 10, 24
salmon 38, 113, **244**, 303
sand 10, 83, 252
satellite 189, **245**, 274
Saturn 221, 264–265, 274
savanna 138, 141
school 160, 202
science **246**
scientist 20, 43, 182, 246
scorpion 83, 169, **247**, 275
sea **206–207**, 304
sea anemone 19, 170
sea bird 13, 140, **248**, 252
sea cow **249**
seagull **140**
seahorse **250**
seal 162, 225, **251**, 256
sealion 251, 256
seashore **252**
season **253**
Second World War 149
seed 116, 118, 170, 223, 238, 239
senses **254–255**
sett 35, 127
shark 112, 208, **256**
sheep station 30, 111
shell 19, 77, 169, 294
shellfish 208, **256**, 279
ship 189, **258–259**
shrimp 208, 250, **260**
sight 254
Sikhs 236
skeleton 151, 153, 169
skunk 35, **261**
skyscraper 29, 49
sleep 142, 143
sloth 93, **262**
slug 263

The publisher would like to thank the following for contributing to the book:

Photographs

AKG Photo 149; **Allsport USA** 276 *r*, 277, 288 *cr*, *bl*; **Andy Teare Photography** 35, 36, 41, 92, 129 *t*, *b*, 144 *tl*, 211 *t*, 212, 215, 247, 261 *t*, 283, 294; **Archiv für Kunst und Geschichte** 26 *b*; © **ARS, NY and DACS, London 1996** 27 *b*; **Bob Thomas Sports Photography** 196 *tr*; **Brian and Cherry Alexander** 21 *bl*; **Bridgeman Art Library** 26 *l*, 27 *tr*, 64 *tr*, 286 *tr*; **Bruce Coleman** 9 *bl*, 166 *tl*, 183 *tr*, 285 *tr*; **Cine Contact** 271 *t*; **Circa Photo Library** 236 *l*; **Colorific** 146 *r*, 203 *l*, 235, 236 *t*; **Dognall Worldwide** 202; **Eye of Science/Science Photo Library** 188 *b*; **Greg Evans International** 149 *m*, 200, 276 *l*; **IBM Eurocoor** 72/73 *t*; **Images** 31 *t*, 203 *r*; **Image Bank** 132 *cl*; **Image Colour Library** 175 *tl*; **Image Select** 147 *r*, 148 *b*; **Lawson Woods** 30; **Liam Muir** 193; **Lupe Cunha Pictures** 32 *r*; **Lyndon Parker** 34, 54, 57, 65 *t*, 74 *t*, 76, 82, 86, 108, 129 *b*, 135, 136, 139, 144 *tr*, 150, 188 *t*, 214, 219, 228, 232, 248, 257, 260; **Mary Evans Picture Library** 120, 184 *cl*; **NHPA** 21 *t*; **NHPL** 29; **Oxford Scientific Films** 23, 25, 33, 43 *cr*, 50, 62, 65 *b*, 69, 74 *m*, 77, 87, 89, 90, 93, 100 *mr*, *ml*, 140 *m*, 154 *b*, 163, 173, 185, 192, 209, 211 *br*, 213, 224, 231, 244, 249, 250, 251, 255 *tl*, 261 *m*, 262, 275, 279 *t*, 311, 313; **Panasonic** 288 *bl*; **Peugeot** 37 bc; **Planet Earth Pictures** 11 *m*, 78, 95, 100 *t*, 140 *t*, 229, 300; **RAC** 116 *tl*; **Renault UK Ltd** 130 *bl*; **Rex Features** 189 *tl*, 230 *cl*; **Robert Harding** 32 *l*, 98 *t*, 101 *cl*, 103 *tr*, 132 *cr*, 174 *cl*; **Ronald Grant** 281 *b*, © 1996 Marvel Characters Inc. *m*; **Science Photo Library** 43 *cl*, 51 *bl*, 72 *tr*, 73 *tr*, 94, 167 *br*, 184 *br*, 186 *c*, 230 *bl*, 284 *tr*, 288 *cl*, 295, 310 *tr*, *br*; **Sony** 298 *bl*; **Spectrum Colour Library** 10, 11 *t*, 31 *b*, 107 *b*, 147 *t*, 148 *m*; **Stephen Hughes/St.Thomas's Hospital** 310 *bl*; **Telegraph Colour Library** 187 *b*, 237 *ml*, 299 *cr*; **Thomas Neile/Hornby** 98 *c*, *bl*; **Tony Stone Associates** 14, 152 *br*, 154 *ml*, 204 *c*, 255 *cb*, 267 *cb*, 268 *bl*, 269 *br*, 287 *cl*, 288 *tr*, 299 *tr*; **TRIP** 21 *m*, 237 *tr*; **Zefa** 107 *t*, 146 *l*, 177 *cr*, 187 *l*, 193, 197 *t*, 198, 206, 233 *b*, 271 *bl*, 305 *m*, *r*, 306, 310 *c*; **Zefa/Ronald Grant Archive** 298 *c*; All other commissioned photographs **Tim Ridley**.

Artists

Graham Allen, Hemesh Alles, Norman Arlott, Mike Atkinson, Craig Austin, Julian Baker, Bob Bampton, Julie Banyard, John Barber, Peter Barrett, Caroline Bernard, Richard Bonson, Robin Bouttell, Maggie Brand, Eric T Brudge, Peter Bull, John Butler, Robin Carter, Lynn Chadwick, Jim Channel, Kuo Kang Chen, Harry Clow, Dan Cole, Stephen Conlin, Rachel Conner, David Cook, Bob Corley, Peter Dennis, Maggie Downer, Sandra Doyle, Richard Draper, Brin Edwards, Michael Fisher, Cecelia Fitzsimons, Eugene Fleury, Roy Flooks, Wayne Ford, Chris Forsey, Rosamund Fowler, Mark Franklin, Andrew French, Terence Gabbey, Michael Gaffrey, Lee Gibbons (Wildlife Art Agency), Tony Gibbons, Mike Gillah, Peter Goodfellow, Ruby Green, Ray Greenway, Craig Greenwood, Peter Gregory, Ray Grinaway, Nick Hall, Darren Harvey, J Haysom, Tim Hayward (Bernard Thornton Artists), David Holmes, Steven Holmes, Adam Hook, Christa Hook, Steve Howes, Biz Hull, Mark Iley, Ian Jackson, Ron Jobson (Kathy Jakeman), Kevin Jones, BL Kearley, Roger Kent (Garden Studio), Deborah Kindred, Martin Knowelden, Mike Lacey, Stuart Lafford, Terence Lambert, R Lewington, Che'en Ling, Mick Loates, Bernard Long, (Temple Rogers), Andrew MacDonald, Kevin Maddison, Mainline Design, Alan Male (Linden Artists), Shirley Mallinson, Maltings Partnership, Janos Marffy, David Marshall (Simon Girling and Associates), Josephine Martin, S McAllinson, Angus McBride, Doreen McGuiness (Garden Studio), B McIntyre, G. Melhuish, Tony Morris, Maggie Mundy Illustrators Agency, Steve Noon, William Oliver, R. W. Orr, Oxford Illustrators, Nicki Palin, Alex Pang, Darren Pattenden, Bruce Pearson, Andie Peck, Bryan Poole, Jonathan Potter, Clive Pritchard, Sebastian Quigley (Linden Artists), Elizabeth Rice, J Rignall, Steve Roberts, Bernard Robinson, Eric Robson, G. Robson, Mike Roffe, Eric Rowe, Mike L. Rowe, Mike Saunders, Liz Sawyer, Peter David Scott, Brian Smith, Guy Smith (Mainline Design), Annabel Spencely, Clive Spong, Paul Stangroom, M. Stewart, Roger Stewart, Treve Tamblin, Myke Taylor (Garden Studios), Simon Tegg, Ian Thompson, Joan Thompson, Guy Troughton, Richard Ward, Ross Watton, T. K. Wayte, Wendy Webb, Lynne Wells, David Whatmore, Graham White, Wildlife Art Agency, Ann Winterbottom, David Wood, Dan Wright, David Wright